Heaps of Trouble

Emelyn Heaps

The Collins Press

First published in 2010 by
The Collins Press
West Link Park
Doughcloyne
Wilton
Cork

British Library Cataloguing in Publication Data

Heaps, Emelyn.
Heaps of trouble.
1. Heaps, Emelyn—Childhood and youth. 2.
Children of alcoholics—Ireland—Dublin—
Biography. 3. Inchicore (Dublin, Ireland)—
Biography. 4. Inchicore (Dublin, Ireland)—Social
conditions—20th century.
I. Title
941.8'350823'092–dc22

ISBN-13: 9781848890411

Typesetting by The Collins Press
Typeset in Goudy Old Style
Printed in Britain by CPI Cox & Wyman

Cover image: poweredge © Debra Lill/Trevillion Images

Heaps of Trouble

EMELYN HEAPS lives in County Clare. At 19, he married and purchased 40 acres of mountain land in Cork. Later he sold the farm, divorced and spent time developing light aircraft. He emigrated to the West Indies in 1988, returning to Ireland in 2001 to build a new life in County Clare in tourism. His hobbies include writing, golf and horse riding.

www.emelynheaps.com

My father's greatest wish was that I would live in interesting times and find true love. He got his wish.
This is dedicated to the person who has been there throughout and spent over two years editing and re-editing my work. Thank you for keeping the faith. The good news is that you have no need to buy book – you probably know it off by heart.

Contents

Renaissance	1
Justifying Sin	19
Goldenbridge versus Hector	35
Christmas Dolls	55
Confessions of an Alcoholic	77
Mayhem and Fireworks	99
Fire and Brimstone	121
A Taste of 'Compo'	149
Fire in the Hole	165
Judgement Day	184
Cupid Strikes	205
Heaps of Trouble	228

Renaissance

THE HOUSE WAS freezing cold, considering it was only early September. The Eastern Health Board had turned off the gas and electricity supplies in their last desperate bid to get me to vacate the empty shop in Inchicore. Their ultimatum made no difference to me anyway, as I had decided it was time to face the hell of moving back in with my parents until I could get a decent job and pay for my own flat.

The previous Friday I had called to see them in their new, semi-detached home in Artane. I had hoped that, somehow or other, things might have changed over the previous six months, particularly since the mother had returned to nursing again. I was greeted by the sight of a 3-foot statue of the Virgin Mary, buried head first in the freshly seeded front lawn. It looked like an unexploded bomb that had been dropped from a great height. Its place of origin and flight path seemed clear, judging by the broken glass of the upstairs bedroom window. Letting myself in by the front door, I could hear the pair of them screaming at each other on the upstairs landing.

'You nearly killed me with that bloody statue, you bitch.'

'I was trying to, you bastard. How could you have forged my name on the cheques you stole from the back of the book? And you thought I would never find out, you thief,' she sneered through clenched teeth.

'There would have been no need if you had not fucked up the court case, killed our daughter and miscarried every one of our babies,' he roared back at her.

Slamming the front door to announce my presence, I climbed the stairs. It was clear that both of them were roaring drunk again and I wondered how the father had got his hands on the mother's cheque book, as she guarded it better than the Pope did his wine cellar.

'Now here's your son back, let him see what sort of life I have with you, you bloody bitch. Come up here and see what your mother has done to me,' he bellowed down at me.

The mother had begun to cry. Before, when I saw her in this state, I could only feel pity for her, even though she had probably started the row in the first place. But after what seemed like a lifetime of watching the pair of them drink themselves stupid, then fight and argue into the early hours of the morning, I had now given up caring.

They were facing each other on the landing and, when I reached the top, I realised this was an argument like no other I had seen before. The father had a large gash on his forehead that was bleeding profusely, but, held very steady in his right hand and aimed directly at the mother's head, was his old First World War service revolver.

'Take another move, Son, and I'll blow her brains out. Look what she has done to me. I think this time the crazy bitch has cracked my skull.' He tentatively felt the wound on his forehead with his left hand and, despite being completely paralytic, his right hand never wavered.

'Look what she did; she threw the bloody statue at me. If I hadn't ducked in time she would have brained me.'

The mother's temper had again flared into a kind of un-controllable madness and, clenching her fists and screwing up her face in anger, she spat the words out at him, 'You bloody bastard, you bastard, you killed Catherine, you bloody bastard.' She began to move towards him.

'This is the last time I'll warn you, you fucking bitch,' the father spluttered, while cocking the hammer of the pistol with a sound of finality that brought the mother to an instant stop.

I caught the mother around the waist and squeezed past her on the narrow hallway, placing myself between the two of them.

'Give me the gun, Dad,' I pleaded.

'I'm going to kill her . . . stand aside if you don't want to get shot . . . now stand aside, I say.'

'Give me the gun, Dad, you don't want to kill anybody,' I said in a trembling voice.

The mother tried to push me out of the way as alcohol rekindled her resolve, saying, 'He won't shoot anybody, he hasn't got the guts, he's nothing but a killer of little children.'

That's just what I need, I thought, one drunken, raving person behind me and another drunken, deranged person with a gun in front of me. For a split second I actually thought he was going to pull the trigger, and I had no idea if the gun was loaded or not. His eyes were bloodshot and he was trembling with temper. Suddenly, overcome with a sensation of calmness that bordered on indifference, I strode forward, reached out and took the gun from him, immediately replacing the hammer and opening the chamber. I began to shake as I found myself looking at the bases of six live shells.

That is precisely how the police found us a few minutes later, no doubt called in by a concerned neighbour. The father was bleeding from a sizeable head wound, I was holding a loaded pistol and the mother was still calling the father every name under the sun, none of them complimentary.

At first I thought they were going to lock me up, as I was the one holding the gun, but the father inadvertently took the

attention away from me when he told the garda to 'fuck off'
and mind his own business. If he wanted to shoot his bitch of
a wife he should be able to do so without having some flat-
footed 'culchie' masquerading as a policeman invading his
home. After confiscating the gun they arrested the father for
causing what they called a 'breach of the peace', and told the
mother and me that we could, if we wanted, attend his court
case the following morning at 10 a.m. in the Four Courts.

On the bus journey the next morning she cried and
reminisced about how much the day's visit to the Four Courts
would upset her, beginning with her usual sympathy-seeking
statement: 'You know, I've had tragedy.'

When she went into that sort of mood there was nothing
else for it but to let her rant on and ignore it. Switch off and
watch the world go by from the comfort of the bus seat, while
wondering if the judge would actually lock the father up.

The father and a guard appeared at ten on the dot in one
of the courtrooms, popping out of a hole in the ground
adjacent to the dock where the court clerk then instructed the
father to stand while the charge was read out. The father
looked the worse for wear after his night in a cell, with his
rumpled suit, unshaven face, sunken hungover eyes and
wearing a bandage on his forehead that one of Napoleon's
Grande Armée soldiers would have been proud to display
during the 1812 retreat from Moscow. Obviously the arresting
sergeant had made sure that he received medical attention
before they locked him up. But with the father you could never
tell if he was play-acting or not. To me, the bandage that was
wrapped completely around his head looked far in excess of
what the wound required. The mother, now she had sobered
up, refused to press any charges, which dampened down the
arresting sergeant's rendition of the previous evening's events.

'Judge,' the sergeant began, while reading from his

notebook, 'we responded to a complaint about a disturbance that was taking place at . . .'

'Stop, stop,' cried the judge. 'Bailiff, what is this man being charged with?'

'Breach of the peace, Judge.' The court bailiff read from a single sheet of paper: 'Damaging private property, displaying threatening behaviour with a firearm, abusive conduct towards a member of the Garda and unlawful possession of a firearm under the Offences Against the State Act.'

'How does he plead?' asked the judge in a voice that suggested he was completely fed up with the day already, even though it was only just beginning.

'Not guilty,' roared the father (before the bailiff could respond) in his clear, strong, English public school voice, 'I wish to represent myself and, as a matter of fact Ma Lud, I also wish to enter a counter-action against the sergeant for breaking and ent . . .'

'Quiet,' thundered the judge, halting the father in mid-sentence, 'you will have your turn to talk soon enough,' and slumped back in his chair. 'Continue, Sergeant.'

'Myself and Garda Murphy, on arrival at the house of the accused, observed a large statue buried head first in the front lawn. It appeared to have been hurled from an upstairs room; we were able to ascertain that from the large hole in one of the windows . . .'

'Objection,' shouted out the father. 'Ma Lud, the sergeant has no proof that the statue was thrown from the . . .'

'Will you be quiet?' said the judge in a voice that now bordered on pleading. 'Please, Mr Heaps, for all our sakes, will you let the sergeant continue? Otherwise we will still be here at midnight.'

'We found the front door ajar and, on hearing raised voices coming from the upstairs, we decided to investigate.

From what we can gather, Judge, the accused attempted to kill his wife with a hand pistol that we have confiscated, and, as was stated by the accused's wife at the time, it was only the timely intervention of their son that averted a possible tragedy. However, Judge,' the sergeant concluded, 'the wife of the accused has now refused to press charges.'

'So then, Sergeant, what are we all doing here wasting the court's time if no formal complaint has been lodged?' enquired the judge tetchily.

'Disturbing the peace, possession of a firearm and abusive behaviour towards a member of the Garda Siochána,' answered the sergeant, seeming amazed at having been asked the question.

'Oh, very well, thank you Sergeant. Well, Mr Heaps, what have you got to say for yourself?'

He gazed straight at the father, who looked like he should have been in hospital instead of standing as the 'accused'. I suspected that he had not been able to get his hands on any drink in the cells the night before and the DTs were probably setting in.

'Your Worship, there appears to have been a great mis-understanding. My wife and I were cleaning the statue of the Virgin Mary when I accidentally fell against it and knocked it out through the window, thus the bump on my head.'

Wow, I thought, now that was good. But there was better to come as he continued, 'As for the rest of the sergeant's allegations, I am at a complete loss, because, Ma Lud, my family and myself were rehearsing for a play when the gardaí broke into my home.'

The onlookers in the courtroom howled with laughter at that statement, as the father gazed at them with a face that implied complete innocence. Even the old judge smiled, as he picked up his hammer and smacked it down to silence the merriment, announcing: 'Firearm to be confiscated. Bound over to the peace for a month and a ten-pound fine. Next case.'

'Ma Lud, Ma Lud,' cried out the father. 'I have not finished, I wish to prosecute the gardaí for breaking and entering into my home.'

'Next case. Bailiffs, kindly escort Mr Heaps from the courtroom.' The father was led away to the sounds of laughter coming from the gallery and the judge shouting for order.

When the three of us met outside, the mother rushed over to the father and examined his head injury while admonishing me over her shoulder: 'How could you do this to us, Emelyn? Bringing shame on us like that.'

'What . . . what are you talking about?' I stammered. 'I didn't do anything. When you lobbed the statue out of the bedroom window the neighbours probably thought you two were murdering each other again and called the guards.'

'We have great neighbours and you shouldn't have called the police, am I right, Ron?'

'You're quite right, Emily.' The father glared at me as though I should have spent the night in prison instead of him. 'Come on Emily, let's find a market pub that's open and I'll get you a drink; I definitely need one after spending a night with the dregs of Dublin society.'

And that was that. The two of them strolled off up the street, arm in arm, the best of friends until the next row, which, knowing them, would probably be later on that evening.

∞

But that was last week, and thankfully I hadn't seen them since. Nevertheless, this night was going to be the last that I would spend in what had been my home for the past seventeen years. The workmen had already begun the transformation of our well-known old toy and sports shop into Inchicore's new Health Centre. However, over the coming weekend at least, my old home would get a short reprieve. As I stared through what had once been our shop's display window, a very early memory of one of the worst hidings that my mother ever gave me came flooding back.

I remember clearly that I was sitting inside the shop, looking out of its large plate-glass window onto a busy street with a crowd staring back at me, laughing. Which encouraged me to make faces at them, which caused more merriment, and therefore motivated me all the more. My mother was across the road gossiping with Mrs Malloy when a customer entering her shop remarked upon the large gathering over the way. This galvanised my mother into racing back to our shop, to discover that I had chosen the front window, right in the middle of a display of toys, fishing-rods and reels, knives and air pistols, to squat down and relieve myself. She promptly interrupted the crowd's entertainment by hauling me out by the scruff of the neck, and then laid into my very bare backside with the cane that she stored under the counter.

The mother was like that: a reactive 'here-and-now' and 'be-damned-to-consequences' type of person. My father, on the other hand, was a more resourceful sort of man and taught me to make sure that I was prepared for any eventuality, something which was to hold me in good stead throughout my teens. To instil this philosophy into me, one day when I was four he brought me to the dispensary where he worked as the Eastern Health Board's Home Assistance Officer for the area. He sat me on the sill of his office window, which was about 6 feet above the ground. Then, assuring me that he would catch me, he encouraged me to jump. Finally, mustering up the necessary courage, I launched myself into thin air and watched with horror as he stepped aside and let me crash to the ground. I lay there bawling my eyes out, nursing my bruised knees and heard him say, 'Never trust anybody, Son, not even your own father.'

He believed in being prepared for any conceivable situation. This attitude had a lot to do with my mother, a bombastic person who ruled the roost with an iron fist. Instead of standing up for himself against her, he would appear to capitulate and resort to quoting one of his favourite sayings: 'Remember Son, there's more than one way of skinning a cat!' This sort of one-sided relationship between my parents had an overwhelming effect on my early childhood. To this day I still hold his attitude partly responsible for one of the major catastrophes that befell our family.

As I stood in the shop that night before leaving it for the last time, my thoughts were inevitably dragged back to the terrible accident. Immediately the smell of burning flesh and hair rushed at me with such an intensity that it threatened to completely overpower me, causing me to gag in an attempt to avoid throwing up. I floundered in the darkness as I tried to be free of the awful memory and stumbled over a crate that the workmen were using as a dining table, knocking the empty cups onto the floor. I came back to reality with a bang and sheepishly realised, that despite the memories swirling around me, my rumbling stomach would have to take precedence. So I decided to escape around the corner to the local chipper.

When I left the shop, it was as if I was seeing the street for the first time; or maybe it was because I knew that I was finally leaving that I was more in tune with its sights and sounds. The Emmet Road of my childhood was similar to any other part of suburban Dublin, in so far as it was comprised of a collection of shops that sustained the necessities of life. It had a post office, food and vegetable shops, a large hardware store, clothing shops, bicycle and toyshops and, of course, a good selection of pubs and chippers. The only blot on the fairly respectable face of the neighbourhood had been Keogh Square – when I was a kid it was probably one of the worst slums in Dublin.

Officially Emmett Road began at Kilmainham traffic lights and, in good old Irish fashion, terminated at the Black Lyon pub where there was another set of lights, making the road about a mile in total. Our shop was in the middle of a new cluster of three 'purpose-built' shops, which were two-storey structures, complete with flat roofs. These shops were bounded by Ward's pub on the right side and, on the left, by what was then CIE's largest bus construction and maintenance yard in the country. The entrance to the CIE compound was off the main road down a narrow street named Spa Road, but their factory sheds took up a large part of the remainder of our side of the road and wrapped around behind the three shops. By the time I reached the age of being able to take note, the large doors of the sheds that fronted the main street had been boarded up with sheets of galvanised iron. The only hint of their original purpose was the rusted tram tracks of a bygone era, appearing from under the main doors like octopus tentacles embedded in the cobbled stones that (back then) covered the length of the street.

The small, concrete backyards at the rear of the shops were divided from each other by 8-foot high block walls, with a 20-foot wall at their rear. These three yards, owing to their walled enclosures, resembled small prison yards and it was only in the height of summer that any sunlight would filter its way in.

Our shop address was 124E Emmett Road, with D and F being to the left and right of us, and it was the only one in the street that did not announce to the world the family name, since the parents had simply called the shop 'Everybody's'. As well as the toys and sports equipment, there was also a drapery section for children's clothing, which sold a great selection of girls' frilly frocks.

From the moment I started school at the age of four I was the envy of every other kid in the street, since they naturally thought that I was allowed to play with all the toys. But, with the strict mother I had, nothing could have been further from the truth, as it was a case of 'you can look, but do not touch'. This was emphasised by a swish of the bamboo cane that she always kept in my view, under one of the shop counters, and of which I was on the receiving end on many an occasion.

There was a bicycle shop at 124D, which was owned by a very tall and thin man called Power. 124F was a vegetable outlet, owned and run by the Finnegans who were originally from the 'country'. The layout of the three shops was identical: on the outside each had two large shop windows on either side of the double access doors. To one side of each of the shop fronts a hall door gave access to the living quarters. An interior door connected the shop to the living/kitchen area, and my mother usually left this open so she could sit and gossip with her friends at the kitchen table or prepare food, while still being able to keep an eye on the shop. Or, when we aspired to a shop assistant, keep an eye on her.

Across the street and slightly to our right stood the Inchicore Workman's Club. The intended use of the building, as the name suggests, was to offer a refuge for the working man on his way home from completing a hard day's graft, and the only entry was through a locked door, guarded by a very diligent porter. The building housed a huge and comfortable bar, complete with one of the first television sets to come into the area, and a snooker room with two state-of-the-art, competition-size tables. Upstairs there was another bar and a very large lounge area where the men could, if they so wished, entertain their wives or lady friends – in the days of my childhood, women were not allowed into bars. Finally, just in case this was not enough, the cellars held yet a third bar and a multitude of dartboards. However, as the place was always packed, morning, noon and evening, somewhere along the way the concept of offering a haven for the hard-working man had clearly been lost. It became a bolt-hole for all the men of the area skiving off work, who knew that once inside its bolted doors they were safe from any person trying to track them down, especially their wives or kids. Needless to say, on moving into the area, my father's first task was to go and join up there.

From a social and pecking order point of view, the most important shop on its side of the road was Malloy's sweet shop. Mrs Malloy was a lady who considered herself amongst the ruling upper class of the street. This self-assumed ascendancy stemmed from the fact that the Malloys were the longest serving shop owners and not 'blow-ins', as the newer arrivals on the street were dubbed. Her claim must have had some impact on my mother, as she spent part of every day visiting and gossiping with Mrs Malloy. At the same time the mother was able to keep her eye on our shop-front door, so that if anybody went in she could bolt across and serve him or her before they had a chance to rob the place blind. But I think the most important factor that enabled Mrs Malloy not only to claim, but also maintain, her position was that her husband was Inspector Malloy of the Gardaí. To have an inspector of the Gardaí living on your street, well, at that time it practically gave you immunity for all crimes committed.

As Emmett Road was one of the main thoroughfares between the capital and the rest of the country, the street was always busy. At all times of the day there was hustle and bustle with people shopping and commuting to or from work. The CIE compound employed a lot of people and the street prospered from having this workforce nearby, especially the pubs. Come teatime, the street would clear as if a curfew had been suddenly imposed, until around ten in the evening when it filled up again with men on their way home from having spent the last few hours drinking away the money earned for that day's toil.

On weekends especially, from my bedroom, I could chart their progress along the street by their singing, which started as a soft murmur, rising to a full crescendo as they drew abreast of our shop, before fading away into the night as they passed on. It was always the same collection of songs, which I learnt off by heart from listening to them so regularly. 'Danny Boy' was the favourite, with 'Kevin Barry' and 'Molly Malone' running a close second and third. Some of the men were quite good singers with clear baritone voices. As they approached the high notes while staggering up the street, they would stop and – with splayed feet, tightly clenched fists, eyes squeezed shut, and their heads flung back – cascade through those top notes on quivering vocal cords. Then they'd continue on their way, as if they had achieved a stunning victory. The odd night a fight would break out, usually while they waited to catch the last bus home at the stop across from our shop. These arguments tended to be more vocal than physical and would continue after they had boarded the bus. I watched their antics from my bedroom window, drawn like a moth to a flame by their raised voices.

'Who are you calling a fecker? You bleeden' fecker.'

'D'ya want a bleeden' clout across the ears, or wha'?'

'Jaysus, you, you and whose bleeden' army?'

And, with that, one of them would try to remove the heavy, CIE-issue coat he was wearing, which would snag around his shoulders and cause a self-inflicted handicap that restricted his arm movements. The two of them would then begin to dance around the bus-stop pole, resembling two fighting cocks shaping up to each other. The one with his arms restrained by the coat would try to keep his balance while attempting to throw punches. At the same time, the other, knowing that his adversary was disabled, would continue to taunt him.

'Come on then, ya old fecker, bleeden' well hit me, then.'

'Jaysus, you just bleeden' well hope that I can't get this bleeden' coat off.'

Eventually the bus would arrive and they would temporarily call a truce while they prepared to board. More than once I saw a bus take off only to screech to a halt a few yards further up, whereupon the two drunks would be catapulted off onto the street by an enraged conductor. The two adversaries, now brothers in arms at the indignation of being expelled from public transport, would vent their rage at the departing bus and continue walking home, arms around each other. From quite a long way off you would still be able to hear their commiserations.

'Fuck, bleeden' CIE's run by a bunch of tossers.'

'Jaysus Mikey, you're bleeden' right there. Haven' I got a cousin working there and he's a right tosser.'

'Feck, is that a fact?'

'Jaysus, did I tell you abou' the time he and his missus called to our house and . . .?' And there the voices would fade away into the night.

When I was still wearing short pants the majority of the population of Inchicore lived in Keogh Square, and the Eastern Health Board dispensary was their only lifeline in respect to social welfare payments and food vouchers. Since the father was the Home Assistance Officer, he alone held the power over who was entitled to these government handouts. The dispensary was a leftover from the time of the British occupation and consisted of a large, square structure enclosed on all sides by a very high stone wall, built to withstand a siege from a determined enemy. Here, also, were housed the doctors, nurses and pharmacy needed to sustain a welfare system on the edge of an impoverished area.

I believe, from what I saw and heard, that the father tried to distribute the funds at his disposal in a fair and equal fashion. Having seen the menfolk of the poorer families wait at the gate of the dispensary and take the home assistance allowance away from their wives in order to squander it on drink, he himself instigated the food-voucher system. Instead of money, the father issued a food voucher that could be cashed at the local shops, but only in exchange for food. He then visited every shop at the end of each week, tallied the amount of vouchers and reimbursed the shop owners with cash.

Frequently, after he had issued the voucher to the wife, an enraged husband would storm back into the dispensary to abuse him and demand money, 'not a fuckin' bit of bleeden', useless paper'. But the father had an aura of authority that would make the most hardened street fighter back down and retreat, mumbling – although the father was not a heavy or large man by any means.

Many a week the local residents laid siege to the dispensary and the father would have to declare a 'state of emergency'. This was a terminology that the staff of the dispensary constantly joked about, as a way of covering up the seriousness of the situation. Wednesday was home assistance pay-out day and often the money did not arrive in time from head office on James Street, resulting in the father, doctors, pharmacists and nurses having to barricade themselves indoors. After many frantic phone calls the arrival of the money or the police – depending on which turned up first – would dictate how the day ended.

If the money arrived quickly, the disturbance would immediately stop and everybody would return to normal as if nothing had happened. However, if the police got there first, the dispensary would remain closed for the rest of the day, until (as the father always put it) 'with the night comes council', and business would resume the following day.

After a while he got smart and, if by eleven in the morning there was no sign of any shillings coming from head office, he would advise his henchman, John, to tell the masses gathered in the large waiting-room that he had been called away on an emergency. Temporarily pacified with this excuse, they would wait patiently while the father slipped out the back door, cranked up his Vespa moped scooter, and drove off to head office to collect the money in person. He would return with the Bank of Ireland moneybags swinging from the Vespa's handlebars, proclaiming to the entire world that he was carrying cash. Back in the 1950s no one dared waylay the Home Assistance Officer, as everybody knew that if the money was 'nicked' that would be that, nobody would get anything, because there would be no more funds forthcoming.

What a conflict of social standards Inchicore was back then; an enigma of contradiction. First there were the shop owners who believed themselves above the rest of the populace and deemed that they were offering the public a service – at their discretion. Then there were the middle-class families who lived out their lives with an Inchicore address; to outsiders the mere name conjured up images of nightly fights, muggings and general bedlam. And, slapped right in the middle of the whole lot, bordered by the canal and Emmett Road, was Keogh Square, one of Dublin's worst slum areas, left to fester and grow by a 1950s government that had no immediate solution for the problem.

As I walked back to the shop with my burger and chips tucked under my arm, I realised that the appearance of our street had not really changed much over the years I had lived there. The CIE compound appeared a bit more run down than previously, but otherwise everything was the same. There was only one significant change: behind the CIE compound the grim reality of Keogh Square was long gone, replaced by the blocks of council flats known as St Michael's Estate.

Re-entering through the hall door, I fumbled my way through the darkness into the kitchen and opened the connecting door to the shop. The street lighting coming through the large shop windows bathed the room with a soft yellow glow and cast deep shadows everywhere.

Christ, I thought, as a moment of panic hit me. I mustn't forget to reclaim Gina's letters, carefully hidden under the floorboards. That was another problem I would have to address. But not right now. There were other issues that demanded my attention before I let in the heartache and the pain that had resulted from losing the only person I believed I could ever love.

As I settled myself down on the floor using the workmen's crate as my table and began to lay out my evening meal, a glint of red on the mantelpiece caught my eye. Heaving myself off the floor, I retrieved what turned out to be a cheap child's bracelet. I was amazed that the workmen had not disturbed it and, more significantly, that the parents not taken it with them. I turned it in my hands and cleaned off the builder's dust, realising that it had remained in that same position for the past seven years. The father had given it to my sister one day, but the mother had turned on him, claiming that he was spoiling her just as he had spoiled me. She made Catherine take it off and leave it on the mantelpiece until such time as

the mother felt Catherine deserved it. Well, she needn't have
bothered, because a few weeks later Catherine was dead.

As I twirled it in my hands, my meal completely forgotten,
back came the recollections and sensations that I had tried to
push away earlier. My chest began to itch, a reaction that
sometimes accompanied the remembered smells of burning
flesh and hair that were never too far away whenever the
memories resurfaced. I strongly resisted the urge to scratch the
scars that covered my chest, because if I opened them up they
could become infected again.

For the first time in seven years I decided to let the past
back in. Maybe it was a fitting time and place to confront my
demons. I sat on the floor with my back against the wall of
what had once been our kitchen. Dim shadows danced and
flickered around the room, caused by pedestrians passing the
shop windows and interrupting the yellow glow from the
streetlights. I closed my eyes and let my thoughts go back to the
very beginning.

Who was responsible for Catherine's death? The father?
The mother? Myself? Or a combination of all three?

So many questions to ask the dancing shadows and ghosts
of the room. Was I the end result of the choices made by one,
or both, of my parents? Was I my own person, capable of
making a future for myself, or had I inherited the
repercussions from their pasts?

Could I say that I had enjoyed my childhood in this
house? Was I mentally capable of reaching back into the past
and laying it out before me? I realised that if I could face these
issues then maybe, on the morrow, I could leave what had once
been my home and face the future with strength and
determination.

Justifying Sin

MY PARENTS WERE married some time during the month of December 1954. Now you may find it strange that I never knew their wedding date, but the simple explanation is that I never heard them talk about it or witnessed them celebrate it. Or maybe they did at the beginning, but by the time I reached an age when I could understand the words 'wedding anniversary' they had already scrapped any celebrations that reminded them of the event.

I am not suggesting that they were always unhappy with each other; it's just that I have great difficulty in remembering a time when they were happy. Perhaps they simply succumbed to the hardship that was survival during the 1950s and 1960s – hardship of which my mother continually reminded me.

In all of the photographs of them taken together before they were married they certainly made a handsome couple. The mother, elegant and slim, had long, blonde hair cascading over her shoulders in the Garbo fashion of the post-war years, highlighting an oval face set off with high cheekbones and a dazzling smile that portrayed an Irish country girl's innocence. The father displayed a stance that spoke of public school and a military career. His features strongly resembled those of the film idol Kirk Douglas, and more than once he used this similarity to its full potential with the ladies.

My mother was born of good farming stock in county Cork in 1921, and was the second youngest of eleven children, of whom six were girls and five boys. I came to know their father as 'D'auld Paddy' (although he was generally referred to as 'Grand Pappy') and he seemed, to me, the epitome of the landed farming gentry. He was well over 6 feet tall, heavy-set, with a frame to match, dressed always in a dark suit complete with buttoned waistcoat and a fob watch. A black bowler hat perched on his thick mane of greying hair and set off a round face that was always close to smiling.

In typical Irish country fashion one son was shipped off to the priesthood and the two eldest sisters were deported to a local nunnery, ending up in a branch in Australia. This was probably D'auld Paddy's way of guaranteeing his place in heaven, while at the same time depleting some of his stock. Two brothers became insurance agents in the county, and the remainder of his children all married into local farming families. Together, they made up a sort of farmers' Mafia that owned a considerable whack of land in the area, with D'auld Paddy as the unofficial Don. All in all, D'auld Paddy must have been quite pleased with his lot; but, as with any large family, there was the usual bitterness between the brothers and sisters as to who got what, and who married whom. Especially on the part of the two brothers who became insurance agents and claimed that they should have been given the home farm, or at least some part of it.

My mother was the exception. At the age of twenty she got on so well with her father that he brought her to the local train station, shoved a twenty-pound note into her hand (together with a one-way train ticket) and told her never to return. That, as far as I know, is how she ended up in London around the end of the Second World War, by then a trained nurse, where, as she said herself, 'I wore the map of Ireland on my face and ran straight into the clutches of your father.'

About my father's family background I am a bit more knowledgeable – or perhaps they were a bit more open in the telling. My grandfather was born Claus, and at the age of thirteen he fled Liverpool (where he had been born) and ran off to join the merchant navy. His voyage of the seven seas ended in a bad accident, which necessitated the replacement of part of his skull with a metal plate. After spending a year in hospital recuperating, he was tossed out of the merchant navy. Now penniless, Claus met up by chance with his brother George in Liverpool at the outbreak of the First World War, during September 1914.

One day shortly after their fond reunion the brothers were sitting around discussing the 'war to end all wars', and contemplating the propaganda that the government was broadcasting. It was being stated that the war would be over by Christmas, which they both agreed was a load of rubbish. They deliberated how to make some money from this bit of world conflict – and the idea they came up with was quite simple.

Regardless of how long the war lasted, the army would need something for the soldiers to sleep on. Why not forget the killing objectives . . . and just give the soldiers mattresses? So they hopped on a train and travelled to London where they met a bemused junior procurement clerk at the War Office. After explaining their idea, they were able to sign a short contract. Short, since (as everybody knew) 'the war will be over by Christmas. What, what, old boy'. By the time they had set up and delivered their first consignment, some bright spark at the War Office had decided that perhaps the war just might drag on a little bit longer than anticipated. Therefore a repeat order was issued – however this time it was substantially larger than the first.

George and Claus were now convinced that the war was

going to continue for several more years. Therefore, they also surmised, the supply of their main ingredient (feathers) would soon start to dry up, particularly since theirs was not the only business supplying mattresses to the army. They decided to source their own feathers elsewhere, to ensure that their little enterprise could continue to flourish. And that is how the Irish connection came into being.

During their first trip to Ireland they succeeded in filling their quota of feathers for the new contract and arranged for direct shipment to their factory in Liverpool, where work was accelerating to meet the heavy demands of the War Office. It was on one of their subsequent visits to Carrick-on-Suir, in southern Ireland, that my grandfather met my grandmother and (after a suitable courting period) they married. That is how my father came on the scene, along with his two other brothers, Stan and Tom.

By the end of the Great War in 1918 George and Claus had become multimillionaires. On the day my father was born Claus enrolled him at Stonyhurst, an English public school. At the age of seven he was deposited at the school doors for what he later described were the worst days of his life. It was a period that he rarely talked about and it was only from the odd snippet that I was able to piece together the family's progression into the hotel business during the late 1920s. Sometimes my father would talk about spending summer holidays in one or more of the many hotels that Claus had bought around England. If the telling of these tales was within my mother's earshot, she would quickly put paid to them by shouting at him to 'stop showing off to the child and stop trying to act the big fellow'. The mother's reaction halted further stories and gave him an excuse (not that he ever needed any) to head off to the local pub or the Workman's Club across the street.

After he left Stonyhurst my father immediately went on to the Royal Military Academy at Sandhurst and was just in time to join up as a captain at the outbreak of the Second World War. By 1946, when he was demobbed, he had, somewhere along the line, been elevated to the rank of major. Once again, the seven years that he served in the British army (described by himself as the period during which he 'assisted Hitler in losing the war') were never spoken about at home. It was after the war, and in England, that my parents met and then returned to Dublin, coinciding with the downfall of the Heaps family empire – an empire that by this time centred on gambling and booze, in that particular order.

During the Second World War Claus sold all of his hotels in England and invested a lot of his money in war bonds. At war's end he moved to Ireland (allegedly with the intention of trying to set up his three sons in business) and purchased a string of betting shops across the country. At one stage he had eleven in Dublin alone. The development of the betting-shop empire coincided with Claus hitting the bottle. To this day I know absolutely nothing about betting shops, bookies or gambling – and, from what I can gather, neither did Claus or his three sons. If they did, they only learnt the business after all of the betting shops had gone bankrupt.

Afterwards my uncle Stan continued as a track bookie and eventually made a successful livelihood from that profession, in spite of a shaky start. Sometimes my father would clerk for him, but these times were few and far between, for whenever the pair of them headed off to the dog track together, inevitably they ended up at a poker game. They would stay out until they had managed to fleece the unlucky sods that had suggested the game in the first place. Add darts, rings and snooker to their list of talents (always played within reach of a bar counter) and you can see why their two wives tried to keep them apart as much as they could.

Alcoholism was one of the main contributing factors that led to the downfall of Claus' empire and the day after he went broke, for some very strange reason, he decided to quit drinking and smoking. The end result was that he and my grandmother moved in to live with us, which put the mother on tablets for a week and sparked off one of the many rows my parents would have on the subject. Years later the mother still brought it up in arguments, declaring, 'Didn't I tell you, Ron, that that mother of yours would be the ruination of us?'

Having the grandparents living with us placed the household under a cloud of gloom and a permanent stress level that affected the mother more than the rest of us. The grandparents moved into one of the two upstairs bedrooms, which they converted into a self-contained flatlet, and then proceeded to contaminate the upper level with strong cooking smells. My mother would scream at my grandmother if she so much as ventured into our kitchen – something that she liked to do on a daily basis, to check on her son's child and to ensure that my mother was feeding me properly. The strain of living with what she described as 'an interfering bitch of a mother-in-law, watching my every step' tended to stretch the mother's nerves to breaking point. Not to mention the fact that my father was spending most of his time in the Workman's Club, boozing and playing snooker. On one occasion, when having a row with the mother, he even announced that he had tuberculosis, to add to her woes.

Being an active child, I decided one fine morning to dismantle the gas stove with an adjustable spanner I had found. This, for my mother, was the final straw in a world that must have appeared to be falling down around her ears. The next day I was marched around the corner, up past Keogh Square, and deposited into Goldenbridge School to enjoy

Sister Charlotte's 'low babies' class. Every day we could hear Sister Ann (through the partition that separated the classrooms) screaming at the kids, with the interruption of slapping noises followed by crying. This struck terror into us all and we thanked God that we were not in her class.

Goldenbridge Convent (as it was officially known) also had an orphanage, situated at the rear of the building and hidden behind railings and gates that the day pupils were never allowed to venture beyond. This only contributed to the horror stories that we told each other about the goings-on inside the place. I believe my father knew that things were not right at the convent. First of all he hated the nuns with a passion. Secondly, since he held the position of Home Assistance Officer for the area, he was also in charge of the dispensary centre at Keogh Square, which had two doctors and several nurses working from it. It stood to reason that the doctors closest to the orphanage had to come from the Keogh Square centre, which was only about five hundred yards away from the school.

One particular evening the father came straight home from work in a foul temper, without first having visited the Workman's Club (definitely a deviation from his usual habit). I was sitting, unnoticed, on the floor in a corner of the kitchen and so I overheard their conversation, which frightened me so much I did not dare mention it again to anybody.

'Those bloody nuns, the lot of them should be placed against a wall and shot.'

'Shush Ron, somebody will hear you.'

'I don't care if the whole street hears me,' said the father, his voice rising, causing the mother to rush over and close the connecting door between the kitchen and the shop, so that the assistant couldn't overhear.

'Two of the sanctimonious bitches came into my

dispensary today, practically hauling a little girl between them, and without so much as a "by your leave" they barged into my office and demanded to see Doctor Dillon.'

'Ron, calm down, what was wrong with that?'

'I felt sorry for the poor little girl, who was as skinny as a lath, so I called Dillon into my office and he carried out a preliminary examination on her.'

The father was shaking with temper and, noticing this, the mother went over to one of the kitchen cupboards, extracted a bottle of whiskey, poured out a liberal amount and handed the glass to him. He continued, after taking a healthy swig from the glass.

'The bloody nuns refused to leave my office as Dillon carried out the examination. One of the bitches even had the gall to turn around and, in a sweet, singsong voice as if butter wouldn't melt in her mouth, announce that poor little Mary must have had a bad fall. Bad fall? The lying twisters, I could see that the little girl had been beaten by one of them. Her little face was swollen, she had two black eyes and her legs and arms were black and blue with bruises. Dillon was furious; he told them that the girl would have to be hospitalised for X-rays, which gave them such a shock I thought they were going to faint. "Oh no, no, Doctor," said one of the nuns, "we couldn't possibly allow that, the Reverend Mother would not be at all happy. All we want you to do is to give us some medication and we will look after her back at the orphanage." "This little girl is going to St Vincent's hospital," Dillon told them in no uncertain terms as he called an ambulance.'

The mother just sat there staring up at him as he finished the whiskey and refilled his glass.

'Of course they refused point-blank to leave her alone at any time in my office, in case the little girl said anything to us, and as soon as the ambulance arrived the two of them climbed into the back with her. And do you know what? They had the cheek to say to me when they were leaving,' and his voice began to rise again, '"we'll say a prayer for you and the good doctor." Can you imagine that? The bloody murdering twisters were going to say a prayer for us, while the two-faced feckers are killing little children behind closed doors and, what's more, being paid by the government to do so. Well, first thing in the morning, I'm going to report the lot of them to the RSPCC.

'Emily, do you know what Dillon told me after they had left?' And, not even waiting for the mother to respond, he continued, 'That he's up there, nearly every week, treating the poor children for some mishap or other. Broken limbs, bruising, scalding and every other bit of misery the nuns can inflict on them. That fucking bastard has known what they have been doing to the orphans for years, and do you know what he had the gall to say to me?

'"Ron," he said, "you are wasting your time thinking that you can change anything. The nuns will justify their actions on the grounds that since the majority of the orphans were born out of wedlock, they are in fact the devil's incarnation, which has to be beaten out of them at all costs." Can you believe that, Emily? And that statement came from one who I thought was an educated man.'

'He's right, Ron,' the mother answered quietly, stunning him into silence. 'Who will believe you? It will be your word against theirs and the church will always win out in the end. All you will do is make us the laughing stock of the neighbourhood. Also you have to think of your son: what do you think will happen to him?'

'I can't believe it, my own wife as well. Are you so afraid of the power of the church that you would remain silent rather than do something about it? Well, the hell with the lot of you, I'm going to expose this barbaric conduct.'

'No, you are not, and if you do I will leave you and take your son with me.'

That was the end of my eavesdropping, because from there it exploded into a fully-fledged row and I slipped out of the kitchen while they were engrossed in shouting at each other. One thing I was certain about: whatever was happening up there, I couldn't believe that it involved Sister Charlotte, since she was nice. As for Sister Ann, well, that was a different matter entirely.

The schoolroom in which I was to spend the next three years was the first in a line of four. The left wall of my classroom ran alongside the street and had a door that led directly out onto the footpath. Sister Charlotte presided over us from a desk that was situated to the left of the large blackboard and was elevated about 3 feet above the floor, so she had a bird's eye view of the whole class. From day one she eliminated any thoughts of misbehaviour, for she could move like lightning. As soon as she spotted and identified any potential troublemaker, she would swoop down from her perch like a black bird of prey and, with a swish of her long ruler, quell even the most troublesome child. The nuns' main role in life, while attempting to bash the three R's into us, was to prepare us for our first confession and Holy Communion; as that date neared the emphasis on religion took priority over the basic fundamentals of teaching us to read and write. My clearest memory of this period (apart from learning my sum tables and being able to write my name down, or copy simple phrases from a book) is of an endless series of mock confessionals. These were conducted with the aid of a screen that lived permanently in the classroom. Sister Charlotte installed herself behind it and, one by one, we knelt at the opposite side and roared out, 'Bless me, Father, for I have sinned and this is my first confession.'

She even went so far as to tell us what sins we had committed, how we should present them to the priest, and in what order, for example: 'Father I've had dirty thoughts.' None of us knew what this meant; however, true to brainwashing stereotype, we figured that we must have had them (and it must be a pretty bad sin), since this was the number one on the list. At first Sister Charlotte tried to get us to recite that we had had 'impure thoughts', but since none of us could pronounce 'impure' properly she gave up and amended this to 'dirty'. She always enforced this statement, while pacing up and down the classroom, by changing her facial expression into a look of absolute piety, pointing to the front of her gown and saying, 'You know, touching yourself down there.' This caused more than one boy to piss in his trousers and he would have to be sent home for the rest of the day. Next in line for major sin-telling in confession was, 'I have said bad words and taken the name of God in vain.' Failure to recite all of these sins in their correct order resulted in the poor 'guilty' kid being placed in a corner for the remainder of the class, complete with a large pointed dunce's hat adorning his head.

The practice for the first communion ceremony was always more fun, as this involved us all lining up in rows and waiting our turn to kneel, in groups, at the front of the class. We had to stick out our tongues as far as they would go and were given a piece of an ice-cream wafer, which the nun had broken down to the same size as the communion wafer that we would eventually receive from the bishop. It was constantly pounded into our heads during this rehearsal that if we were to let the wafer drop out of our mouths during the real event we would be committing a mortal sin. For this was the 'body and blood of Jesus our Saviour', and the shame involved in picking the wafer up from the floor of the church was far too great to contemplate. As for the culprit, well, he would be doomed for

eternity into the fiery pits of hell. It was amazing the effect this
threat had on some of us: we would concentrate so hard on
keeping the piece of wafer balanced on our tongues that the
nun would have to tell us to close our mouths and swallow.

During the winter, when the heating was turned on, head
lice rampaged unchecked amongst the pupils. I had a mop of
wavy blond hair and the mother (who didn't want to cut off
my curls) produced the louse comb every evening when I
arrived home and proceeded to remove the nits that had taken
up residence during the day. Having succeeded in dodging the
delousing ritual for a few days, I passed the grandmother in
the hall one evening, whereupon she noticed that I had fleas
and lice leaping from curl to curl. This set the whole
household in uproar, as she dragged me around like a sack of
spuds and screamed at the top of her voice that once the fleas
were in the house we would have to burn the place down to get
rid of them. And hadn't poor Claus seen enough of them to
last a lifetime during his mattress-making days, as turkey
feathers were full of them? And what was the mother doing
allowing me go around with a head full of lice and making a
show of them? What was her Ronny going to say when he got
home? While she roared all this out she was filling up the
kitchen sink with hot water to execute the kill.

The mother had to endure all of this ranting from the
shop front where she was serving customers – who, by this
time, were backing out of the door in case they, too, became
infested. She tried to tell them that the grandmother was going
a bit batty and, in any case, the fuss was about our dog. That
evening my curls were chopped off by my father with a brand
new pair of hand shears, especially purchased for the task. I
was not allowed near a barber's shop because, according to my
mother, they never washed any of their combs and I would
end up with a fresh load of fleas for our troubles.

From that day on bags of DDT powder were purloined weekly from the dispensary by the box-load and sprinkled liberally around the house – especially in the beds, because my grandmother insisted in showing off every real and imaginary fleabite that she had acquired during the night. I was kept from school until my mother had had a chance to talk to the Reverend Mother; the father refused to go anywhere near the convent, since he was still adamant that he was not going to let the 'twisters' get away with beating up orphans. I eventually returned to school, minus blond curls and reeking of head-lice repellent.

A short time after that episode, at school one morning, it was clear that something major was in the air. The nuns were all babbling together in groups, clapping their hands and smiling as if the Second Coming had been announced. Actually, for them, it was the next best thing, for the news that caused them so much excitement was that the Pope was coming to visit Ireland. Scrap teaching the three R's again and put first confessions and Holy Communion on hold; the business in hand now was to teach us everything we should know about Pope John XXIII – and to throw in a full history of the previous twenty-two Johns for good measure.

The Pope's forthcoming visit was perceived, by media and clergy alike, as if Ireland had been singled out especially by the Vatican: it was a sign from heaven that we, the Irish, were due to prosper. Well, this certainly worked in our case, for the father was not one for letting an opportunity pass him by. He promptly went in to Hector Gray's wholesale shop on Liffey Street and bought up their entire stock of papal flags and bunting, which he sold as fast as he could load them on to the shop shelves.

A week before the visit the whole street went into a frenzy trying to outdo each other with decorations. We had flags flying from every upstairs window; the bunting linking our shop to Coleman's clothing shop across the road was taken care of by the 21A bus on its first passing.

The day of the Pope's visit finally arrived and, as school-kids, we probably knew more about the Pope than he did himself. We spent the morning in class receiving last minute instructions from the nuns on how we were to conduct ourselves; this instruction included two visits from the Reverend Mother, who appeared as fussed as if she was about to spend her first night in bed with a man. Then we were finally marched off in tightly packed columns, flanked and patrolled by nuns to the left and right of us, to ensure that no child tried to sneak off home. Even the orphans were let out that day and took up the rearguard. At the head of some two hundred shuffling kids, all bound to silence by fear of retribution the next day if caught talking, strode the Reverend Mother with her long black robes swishing and blowing in the wind.

We marched down Emmett Road, then turned into Tyrconnell Road and were marched past St Michael's Church towards the junction that joined Kilmainham to the Canal. We were headed for a stretch of footpath that, by prior arrangement, had been left free for our arrival. It seemed that every other school in Dublin was lined up as far as the eye could see. The majority of children clasped little papal flags mounted on thin bamboo sticks, which had a tendency to break if waved too vigorously and were completely useless for poking your companion in the sides. The flags had been ceremoniously issued by the nuns, with the strict instruction that they had to be returned the next day.

We waited for hours by the roadside and the tension mounted with every passing minute as the afternoon wore on. It seemed to get hotter and hotter, with the road dust blowing up around our knees at every gust of wind. The nuns patrolled up and down the lines getting us to recite the rosary, and repeated over and over the same instructions: as soon as He arrived we were all to bless ourselves, frantically wave our flags and cheer, and all at once.

False alarms were frequent and usually started by some gurrier shouting, 'Jaysus, he's coming, he's bleeden' coming, look.' Which had us blessing ourselves, flag-waving and screaming our heads off until the nuns, arms flapping and running wildly up and down the road, shouted at us to 'shut up this minute'. The Reverend Mother would then hold a meeting with all of her flock to see if they could identify the offender.

We had almost given up any hope of him coming, and sheer boredom had beset the children to the point that the nuns let us sit down on the curb of the footpath before half of us collapsed from fatigue. Suddenly, without any warning, two police motor bikes roared past and, before the nuns could galvanise us into the blessing-ourselves, flag-waving and cheering mode, a very large, jet-black car zoomed past. We could barely make out the vague silhouette of some fellow dressed in white, waving and making the sign of the cross at us, but it had the nuns throwing themselves to their knees and blessing themselves as if it was the end of the world. And that was that; at the rate the car was moving, the Pope must have been in a hell of a dash to visit all of Dublin in the quickest time possible. It was many years later (after a discussion in a pub involving the whole of that night's clientele) that I finally had to accept that it was only the Pope's second-in-command, the Papal Nuncio, who had visited Ireland at that time.

During that year, the father traded in the moped, which been our family's mode of transport, and invested in a brand new Ford Popular motor car, duck-egg blue in colour, at a cost of £500. This made us the envy of the road, as we were one of the few families on the street to possess a car. It also had the effect of elevating the mother to the role of chief mechanic and back-seat driver; she never allowed the father to drive over 35 miles an hour. After every 50 miles or so, she insisted on stopping at a pub to allow the engine to cool down. These were the worst parts of any journey, as children were not allowed into pubs then and I had to wait in the car, sometimes for hours on end, while the car was 'rested'.

Having the car opened up a completely new lifestyle for us, as relatives could be visited, both on my mother's and father's side, instead of waiting for them to come to us first. Also, the father joined Newlands Golf Club at Newlands Cross, and he often frequented Wang's restaurant on the Naas road on his way back from golfing. My grandmother could now be deposited with ease for visits to her two sisters in Carrick-on-Suir, especially important because my grandfather had just recently died. A fact I hadn't been aware of at all, since my mother insisted that young children had no business being introduced to funerals at too early an age.

Goldenbridge versus Hector

ONE OF THE advantages of going to Goldenbridge School was that it gave me the opportunity to meet other children of my own age. However, any potential new friend of mine was closely vetted by my mother. She posed questions to the new playmate in a manner that would have pleased even the staunchest Gestapo officer, and always followed the same format: 'Where do you live and what does your father do?' If the poor fellow answered with an address, or a parental occupation that did not fit in with my mother's preconceived notion of suitability, well, that was that. He would end up being unceremoniously hunted from our doorway and I would be dragged inside and given a housekeeping task that involved anything from washing-up to sweeping the floor. It was this snobbish approach that ensured that I didn't have very many friends at all, which made me a loner, preferring my own company to going through the bother of trying to get a new acquaintance approved.

As for the parents, they had a broad spectrum of visitors who constantly streamed in and out of the house. Most were people that my father had befriended, either in his job or through the local branch of the Fianna Fáil Cumann. He felt that being a member of the only political party that had always been in power and would continue to be re-elected ('Who the hell would ever vote for that other lot of wasters?') would be good for our business. Since the shop remained open until late in the evening, the lights of the front windows attracted visitors as moths to a flame and our kitchen turned into a sort of 'halfway house'. I never knew the real names of these people, for the father christened each and every one of them with nicknames that he used when talking about them to the mother.

Boy-o-Boy was a teacher at the local technical school and on average he called in two or three times a week on his way home. I was five years old the first time I met him, and the enduring memory I have of him is that I can't ever recall seeing the man sober. He frightened the life out of me, for he was a tall man with a long, black coat that he never took off, which had several inner pockets well stocked with a variety of whiskey, gin and brandy bottles.

On one particular evening my father heard the knock at the hall door, recognised the tall shape silhouetted against the frosted glass as the streetlights magnified his shape and cast his long, exaggerated shadow down our darkened hallway, and ducked out of sight. He told me to open the door and tell Boy-o-Boy he was not at home. Me, I promptly forgot the last request, being too young to tell lies (if I had, I would have been bright red the following morning at school when my conscience forced me to confess to Sister Charlotte during the communion rehearsals). I just opened the door and let him in without saying a word. The father, realising that I had not carried out his instructions, knowing that he could be heard, and certainly not wanting to appear inhospitable, called out to me to 'open the door and let our guest in'. Boy-o-Boy stood swaying from side to side in our hallway. Focusing on me, he glared into my face with bright red, bloodshot eyes, causing me to recoil rapidly. I had never smelt anything so bad in my life.

Then he belched once and said, 'Well, Ronny boy, at least he can be proud that he was born in a free state,' before belching again and promptly falling over. After my parents had picked him up and deposited him in an armchair by the fire, he conjured up a bottle of whiskey from under his coat. I was mesmerised at this stunt, thinking that he was some sort of a magician, and was further impressed that his fall had not broken the bottle, as he had fairly hopped off the concrete floor. He then liberally filled the half-pint glasses that my father had produced (in anticipation of Boy-o-Boy's generosity with booze and his need for a stiff drink after his fall) and insisted that my mother join them. He would not let my father touch his drink until another glass was found. This he also filled to the brim before handing it to my mother, who was sitting down in the armchair across from him on the other side of the fireplace. She was still officially tending shop from her armchair, but knew that a refusal was futile, so she waited for her opportunity when he turned to face the father. Then she dashed the contents of the glass into the fire, causing an unexpected explosion. A whoosh of blue flames roared out from the hearth like a rocket launching and blew Boy-o-Boy out of his seat and halfway across the floor. He landed without spilling a drop of his whiskey and, picking himself up with the father's assistance, uttered 'Boy, oh boy, Ron, but this is strong stuff,' before falling over again.

My hero was 'Shady Steven', a regular caller to our shop; considering he was only in his twenties, he was certainly out of character with all of the other visitors who were generally the same age as my parents. I never saw him but he wasn't smiling and every birthday, no matter what the parents gave me, it was always Steven's present that I looked forward to receiving. He would arrive with the most astonishing boxes of Meccano sets that you could possibly imagine. When Lego came out, well, this opened up new boundaries of imagination; each year he would remember what he had given me the year before and expand on the set.

Not-My-Round Jim always called at the weekend along with his wife. He earned his nickname by constantly trying to dodge buying a round of drinks, especially if he found himself in a large gathering. 'Ambush Tom' had earned his name during the Irish Civil War by setting up an ambush somewhere in the Wicklow Mountains and netting, as a prize, a busload of priests and nuns heading off to a 'retreat'. When he and his men were threatened with instant excommunication from the Catholic Church for interrupting their travels, Jim had had to supply them with an escort to see them safely to their destination.

∞

It was during this period that my mother became pregnant again and the serious rows between my parents began in earnest. Most of them started with the father arriving home late from work and bringing with him, either individually or all together, his drinking partners Boy-o-Boy, Not-My-Round Jim or Klepto Joe. As I would have been hunted to bed hours before, I would hear the father's arrival, the ensuing period of merriment, and the final slam of the hall door announcing the departure of the guests. Creeping to the top of the stairs, I would wait for the row to begin. My grandmother, who was still living with us, would stand in the doorway of her room until the slamming of doors downstairs heralded the impending arrival of my father upstairs. Which would put me running back to my room, diving under the covers, and faking sleep – but still able to hear my grandmother's comment to my father, 'Ronny, is she at you again?'

These fights placed an umbrella of gloom over our

household. The worst part was not the rowing, since this only lasted for a few hours, but the days of silence between my parents, which turned all mealtimes into sullen gatherings. The silence was broken only by the scuffle of my grandmother's feet across the lino flooring in the kitchen as she passed. On one particular day my mother had just washed the floor and covered it with old newspapers to stop dirty feet spoiling her handiwork. It was just after lunch and an exceptionally lengthy period of silence between my parents. The grandmother chose that time to shuffle past the table, dragging all of the newspapers up in her path. This resulted in the mother exploding with pent-up rage. Flying off her chair, she started to emulate the grandmother's actions across the floor, scattering newspapers in all directions with her feet, before hunting her out of the kitchen and down the hallway. The father got up from his chair, where he had remained silent throughout the whole episode, and quietly walked out of the house. Seeing this, I too hopped up and followed him up the street towards the dispensary. He completely ignored me, so I waited outside on the steps until he came out at around five in the evening and followed him across the road to the Workman's Club. Eventually he came up to me and informed me that he was finally going 'to leave that bitch of a mother of yours'.

Being only five, I thought this was going to be the best adventure of my life and I begged him to take me with him, convincing him that I was worthy with statements such as, 'I can't live with the bitch, either'. He decided that I could accompany him and, after he had installed me on a barstool, informed me that he was going to make arrangements for our escape just as soon as he had finished a 'quick game of snooker'. My imagination sparked with visions of boat trips over the Irish Sea, long journeys across England fraught with danger while my father searched for employment, finding new friends and places to visit, and (possibly) finally meeting my father's relatives. I sat and dreamed of adventures unknown.

As the hours ticked by and more and more men came to fill up the bar (the father was finishing yet another 'quick game of snooker'), my visions of great adventures diminished. Finally, at around ten that evening, my father collected me from my perch, led me out of the door and began walking away down the road in the direction of St Michael's Church, with me skipping after him and still hoping that our journey was about to begin. He went straight into a small corner shop that was still open and purchased two tins of tomato soup, a loaf of bread, butter and some cheese.

Leading me by the hand, he brought me back to his office in the dispensary where he turned a small, two-bar electric fire over on its back. He then butchered open the tins of soup with a surgical scalpel he had acquired from one of the doctor's day rooms. He proceeded to heat up the soup, still in the tins, causing the labels to singe and smoulder before finally igniting. While the soup was 'warming', he toasted the bread, applying liberal quantities of butter and cheese. Finally we settled down at his desk to devour the hastily concocted meal. As soon as we had finished, he suggested that perhaps we should postpone our departure until the next day. When we finally snuck back into the house well after midnight, he put me to bed with instructions to say 'not a word about this to that old bitch', and suggested that we should leave as soon as I came home from school the next day.

Within two days some form of normality had returned to the house and the parents were beginning to exchange words again, which coincided with my mother's announcement that her father was coming to visit. My small bedroom was going to be turned over to him and I was to move into the grandmother's room. Grand Pappy, who at this time was well into his seventies, always enjoyed his visits to Dublin and would walk daily into O'Connell Street. Each day, when he returned, he would take me out for a walk, either up along the canal or in the opposite direction to Memorial Park or the Phoenix Park.

During these walks Grand Pappy would ply me with vast amounts of chocolate (totally against the mother's strict instructions). Inevitably I ended up covered with melted chocolate and, rather than face the wrath of the mother, he would drop me at our door and skive off in search of my father. Over a drink Grand Pappy would commiserate with the father regarding the mother's temperament and explain why he had given his daughter a one-way ticket off the farm in the first place. My father never missed an opportunity, when having a row with the mother, to remind her of these conversations he had with her own father. And he constantly provoked her by telling her, 'If your own family can't put up with you, then why the hell should I?'

But the visit Grand Pappy made to us after the electric fire feast was to be his last. Finally the simmering issue of the one-way ticket exploded into a blazing row between the mother and the grandfather. I recall my father driving him for the last time to Kingsbridge Station to catch the train to Cork. As we arrived at the door of his compartment, Grand Pappy reached into his waistcoat pocket, extracted a half-crown coin and, turning to me, pressed it into my hand. A whole half crown: I was rich beyond belief and it was all mine. On the way back home I kept staring at it to make sure that it didn't dissolve.

Even though the grandfather had returned to Cork, I was not allowed to move back into my old room. Instead the mother converted it into a small, upstairs living-room. Once it was decked out with new furniture, I was never allowed back in there, which I felt defeated the purpose of having the room in the first place. I was told that it was to be used only for entertaining 'special guests' – which I took to mean her brothers and sisters and the local parish priest. Also, according to the mother, my father's 'lot' was never going to set foot in that room.

∞

It was approaching Christmas and, as I was now nearly six and had given up believing in Santa Claus, the father thought I was old enough to be introduced to the ways of the business world and to bring around the wholesale outlets in Dublin. Now it was not the case that I had stopped believing in Santa as a result of my own process of logical thought. It was just that one day the father took me aside and told me that it was a load of made-up rubbish and that, in fact, all the toys for the kids in our area were bought in our shop. But, he warned, I wasn't to tell any of the other children that I came in contact with, as this bit of news could ruin our business.

To me, visiting the wholesalers was like discovering the New World. There was Millard Brothers on the quays, which supplied our fishing-rods, tackle, knives and, most importantly, guns of all descriptions. There were pellet guns of every make and size, from repeater rifles that looked identical to the Winchester rifles all the cowboys carried in the films, to hand pistols that fired all sizes of pellets. And there, standing shoulder to shoulder in the long gunroom (which appeared to be carved out of oak beams), were rows and rows of real guns, from rifles to shotguns and everything else in between. As soon as I entered that room, the smell of gun oil seemed to overpower my senses and set every fibre of my body tingling with excitement. I stared up at the racks of weapons that conveyed power, strength, and gave off an aura of potential, awesome destruction. Turning towards the aisle that ran the length of the floor, I saw endless stacks of large boxes containing packets of every kind of bullet imaginable. I lifted one small packet (which seemed to weigh a ton), carefully opened the top, and there, glaring out at me, were the polished tops of .22 calibre bullets. They looked so perfect and of such faultless beauty that I felt it would be criminal to even think of firing them. The smell of gun oil seemed to penetrate the very pores of my skin, lingering with me for weeks on end. So much so that, in later years, every time I entered the gunroom at Millard Brothers the same feeling came rushing back.

Entering Hector Gray's on Liffey Street was akin to entering Aladdin's cave, since the two storeys were filled to the brim with every sort of toy you could imagine. I was welcomed by old Hector himself and told that, since it was my first visit, I could choose a present for myself. I had such a huge choice that I could settle on none, for as soon as I spotted some toy of tremendous interest I would find something else and run off to look at that, until another would catch my eye.

The father was engrossed in haggling prices with Hector when a very tall old gentleman with a mop of white hair and a long white beard, who had been sitting quietly in a chair in a corner of the shop, called me over and enticed me to sit with him. If I had still believed in Santa, well, this would have been him; he was just short the red coat and black boots. Introducing himself as Noel and sitting me on his knee, he told me a story about a whale called Moby Dick. In a rich Dublin accent he entranced me with his tale of the sea captain who spent a lifetime in search of a white killer whale that had eaten his leg. It was some years later that I associated my memory of the storyteller with the well-known actor Noel Purcell, recalling also that he featured in the film *Moby Dick*, which was made in Youghal, County Cork, in the late 1950s.

That week leading up to Christmas was the most exciting of my young life to date, as we had to make frequent trips to the wholesalers – mostly owing to the fact that we had a large shop and a small car that could only hold a little at a time, despite my father's attempts to jam in as much as he possibly could. There was many a trip home that found me sitting on top of boxes stacked on the front seat, my head jammed up against the roof. I would be given strict instructions to watch the boot, as this too would have been overfilled and tied down with string. Hector's shop was always the last port of call, being the one place that doled out generous quantities of alcohol to all its customers.

By the time we had completed the ordering and loading, nearly everyone in the shop was well on their way towards complete inebriation, both staff and customers. I could always tell when the father was reaching his limit of consumption, as his ordering slowed right down and he concentrated more and more on the booze table. Until eventually Hector or Enda presented the full bill, which was haggled over; once they came to an agreement the father would reach into his back pocket and extract a bundle of five- and ten-pound notes. To me the notes appeared to be as large as newspapers and he would make a great show of counting out the tally. However, nobody really wanted to leave with plenty of half-empty bottles of booze still lying around like magnets (especially magnetic to the father), so the customers would encourage Hector to tell one of his stories about his start in business. Hector, if he had made a lot of money that particular day, would refill their glasses and reminisce about what he described as 'the good old days before the taxman found me'.

'Every Sunday,' Hector would begin, launching into one of his favourites, 'I took a patch down on Moore Street, where

I set up my stall and flogged to the masses anything cheap that I could get my hands on. In those days the crowds descended on the street around noon, with their wives and girlfriends attached to their arms.' At this point all work in the shop would stop and the staff would angle over to hear the rest of the tale. 'Well, this particular time, I got my hands on a gross of some very cheap "magic Japanese soap" that was supposed to remove every conceivable stain from any type of clothing . . . it didn't work, of course, but since I was stuck with it, well, I had to sell it on.' Turning around in mock modesty he would raise his arms in the air and say, 'Well, isn't that what all good Jew boys are taught to do by their fathers?', which brought roars of approval from the gathering.

'Knowing that it would barely remove fly shit from a black shirt, I had to be a small bit creative and sort of "invent" my own dirt that the soap could remove, otherwise I would have been eating the bars for my Christmas dinner.' At which point one of the group would remind Hector that, as he was a Jew, he shouldn't be celebrating Christmas anyway – which brought more laughter, but Hector would continue unabated.

'Old Bob who had his stand alongside mine flogged rags that he passed off as cloths, and which he bought from the Jew boys on the North side . . . and he always arrived early with his horse and cart and parked his wagon next to my patch. Experimenting at home with the bloody stuff, I realised that if I mixed soot with ground-up soap bars it looked like grease and, mixing it into a paste, I could apply it to any piece of cloth . . . and lo and behold the "magic Japanese soap" would remove the stain. The next Sunday I arrived early to coincide with Bob's arrival and, after carefully removing all of the grease from the back axle of his cart wheel, I reapplied my own invention, then set up my stand and awaited the arrival of the punters.'

You could have heard a pin drop at this stage and the

arrival of a last-minute customer was met with frantic hand
signals telling him to be quiet and to come over and join the
company.

'Well, before long,' continued Hector, after acknowledging
the new arrival with a nod of his head, 'I had a crowd circling
me and, after describing the amazing magic quality of the
Japanese soap, the moment of truth arrived and, stepping off
my box, I cried out that it would even remove axle grease.
Reaching down to Bob's wagon I removed a handful of my
special paste, smeared it on the front of my white shirt and, to
everyone's amazement, the bar of soap removed the stain
before their very eyes. With the crowd expanding, I got carried
away and started to smear the "grease" onto some of the male
onlookers' shirts, which first brought cries of indignation from
their lady friends . . . but as soon as the stain was removed,
gasps of amazement. Making me, there and then, on the spot,
decide that I was not charging enough for the stuff and I
should double the price of it.'

Cries of 'shame, Hector that's not like you' came from the
gathering, which was at this stage liberally helping itself to his
booze. Hector, grinning from ear to ear, informed them that
he could not take the money from the punters quickly enough
and, holding his hands up for silence, he added that he was
not quite at the end of the story yet.

'The next Sunday morning, arriving early again and
loaded down with the remaining boxes of the soap mix, I
repeated the stunt with Bob's wagon. It was raining slightly,
so I decided to take shelter in Milligan's pub until it cleared
and to await the arrival of the normal Sunday punters there.

'Afternoon, with the streets filling, I ambled back to my
stand and, as on the previous week, before long I had a large
group gathered around me. This time, to create a bigger
impact, I picked out of the masses the biggest and ugliest

docker that I could find. Calling him up to the stand, I once again ducked under Bob's cart and, with a handful of my special grease, smeared it onto the front of his starched white shirt, his Sunday best. With the size of the man, it was like applying it to the side of a ship and his little woman nearly fainting with the shock of what I was doing.'

Here Hector paused and hung his head, as if he was reliving the moment, and everybody else held their breath in case he would not finish. But after a few seconds he again raised his head, smiled that huge grin of his at the assembly and, to the sound of sighs of relief being expelled all around him, he continued.

'Climbing back on top of my box, for the bastard was so tall . . . even on my box I only came up to his chin . . . his face was getting redder and redder, and me grinning up at him like the village idiot. At the same time at the top of my voice telling him and the crowd not to worry, and fighting off his missus who was tugging at my arm demanding to know how she was going to wash it off and who was going to pay for a new shirt? I proceeded to apply the "magic Japanese soap" to his barrel chest, whilst anticipating the cries of amazement from the masses and, more importantly, the animal in front of me. Well, to my great astonishment, nothing happened – and the more I rubbed with the soap, the more I spread the black crud around his chest area. Finally, it dawned on me that I was, in fact, spreading real axle grease all over the chest of one of the largest gorillas in Dublin.

'Dropping the bar of soap in fright, I was just in time to duck out from under the two large, shovel-size hands that were reaching out in my direction . . . and leaping off the box, I fled in terror down Moore Street. The yells of the docker filled my ears, claiming that if he ever caught up with me he would tear me limb from limb.'

With howls of laughter reverberating around the shop, Hector finished his story by informing us that he was not able to go back to Moore Street for quite a while, as every Sunday the docker came in search of him. It was only months later, when he finally met up with Bob again, that Bob was able to explain to him that on that famous Sunday morning somebody had borrowed his wagon and, with the space vacant, another person had parked theirs next to Hector's pitch.

The story was still ringing in my ears as we finally left Hector's shop, the father staggering out to the now fully loaded and trussed-up car. We began our journey home through the thickening fog, past the Four Courts, Kingsbridge Station, up to Kilmainham, and finally into Emmett Road. The shop was lit up like a lighthouse, with the yellow gleam from the windows piercing through the fog. Adding to the glow and illuminating the wide footpath outside the shop entrance were the flickering, multicoloured fairy lights that surrounded both windows and appeared to blend into the orange luminescence of the streetlights, emitting a welcoming aura of safety and warmth.

The two shop doors were flung open and the contents of the car stacked in the middle of the shop floor. This was to be my first introduction to the art of 'creative' pricing, rather than the more boring method of applying a standard profit mark-up across the board. The mother would hold up an item for the father to consider, while she read out the cost price from the wholesale price-list in her other hand. Together they then debated what they could get for it. Once decided, the mother used a heavy black marker to write the sale price on all the boxes before storing them on the shelves and placing one aside for display in the shop window.

The morning of Christmas Eve finally dawned and for the first time I was going to be allowed to take part in the shop's activities: I was to be the fetcher and carrier of the items to be wrapped for the customers. By ten in the morning, the kitchen was cleared of all furniture except the table (which was dragged out into the middle of the room) and the sideboard (loaded with bottles of booze, including a special bottle of orange for me). Large rolls of brown paper were stacked by the table, along with boxes of sellotape and, for the customer who wanted to pay extra, special sheets of Christmas wrapping paper that cost three pence more.

Every shelf in the shop was overflowing with toys and rows of two-wheel bikes, three-wheel trikes, teddy bears of all sizes, toy prams and plastic pedal cars were suspended from hooks in the ceiling. Whirling under them, attached by pieces of string, were large, cardboard signs displaying their prices.

By eleven o'clock, as I looked out at the street beginning to fill up with pedestrians, I could almost see the excitement shimmering in the air. It was intensified by the greetings that the women called out to each other as they passed, fuelling the atmosphere with their exhilaration. At first, thoughts of the Christmas dinner were foremost in the shoppers' minds, and the line of turkeys, hanging in the butcher's window across the street, started to diminish. Then, like a changing tide, the emphasis on food subsided and the masses began to move over to our side of the street to commence the first flurry of present buying. This first wave, led by the women, receded around lunchtime; it was then as if the street were drawing breath for the main event that would not begin until about four in the afternoon, when the menfolk returned home from work.

By early afternoon our 'helpers' began to arrive, in the form of the father's friends, complete with wives and girlfriends. The women took up station in the kitchen area and began to lay out the materials required for wrapping presents, almost as if they were surgeons awaiting the first casualties to arrive from a war zone. The father, having assessed their sales skills, positioned each of the men carefully around the shop floor. He himself took a slightly elevated position on the step between the shop and the kitchen, just like a general overseeing the battlefield. Here he was ready to rush to the assistance of any area that looked as if it was about to be breached by frantic shoppers.

Shady Steven, posted down by the sporting section, had a proficient knowledge of fishing and shooting, and could (according to the father) 'sell condoms to the bloody nuns'. Not-My-Round Jim was set up halfway along the toy shelves, as he had a gentle face that would overpower even the most hardened shopper. Considering all of his family were long grown up and Jim hadn't a clue about toys (or, if he had had one, it was now only a distant memory), he could sell any toy to any person, regardless of what they had originally come in to purchase.

Klepto Joe was out in the middle of the shop floor ready to take down any item attached to the ceiling and pass it in for wrapping. The father needed to keep him as far away as possible from behind the counter, as Joe had two problems that had manifested themselves over previous Christmas Eves in the shop. One, he was a compulsive gambler, which to a certain extent did not interfere with Joe's assistance in the shop; but the other problem did, as he was a kleptomaniac. He could not help 'storing' any item that would fit into his pockets and the father was not going to give him the opportunity to feck any of our stock if he could help it. Since Christmas Eves at 'Everybody's' were by now a ritual that went back to the shop's beginnings, the father could not refuse his assistance without explaining the reason; and since Joe was also his drinking buddy, well . . .

Another Jim, who only appeared at Christmas, was

completely useless at selling anything, setting the father a real challenge in keeping him out of the way, while at the same time making him feel that he was performing an important task. So he placed him in 'overall charge' of the wrapping section. Which translated into his doing nothing, but still thinking that he was doing something important. And since he was in the same room as Boy-o-Boy, the two of them could drink themselves silly.

As for Boy-o-Boy, he took up residence by the drink table and was ready to hand out a glass of whiskey to anybody who felt the need of revival. Because he also came with his own stock of booze secreted about his person, there was never a chance of running out.

Finally there was the mother, located by the cash register with her two lady shop assistants who were in charge of the children's clothing section. Throughout the evening she bundled up rolls of banknotes and handed them to the father who stuffed them into the pockets of a pair of very baggy pants that he wore specially for the occasion. So that, by the end of the evening, with front and back pockets bulging, it looked as if he was wearing a pair of Spanish Conquistador pantaloons.

By five in the afternoon the full force of the shoppers had descended on the store; by six the two front doors had to be taken off their springs and tied back to allow the hordes of people trying to get in and out to pass. The bright lights of the shop illuminated every corner and the constant ringing of the till announced yet another sale, mingling with the curses and cries of the people trying to get attention. All you could see of Joe was his hands raised high above his head as he forced his way through the press of people to hand over some object for wrapping to the ladies in the kitchen (who were now working at a feverish speed in an attempt to keep up).

I raced between the legs of the people behind the counter

delivering goods for wrapping, and then gathered up the wrapped parcels for delivery back to the customer. Boy-o-Boy was diligently handing out drinks to everybody behind the counter and, each time he passed the father, he muttered, 'Boy, oh boy, Ron, but it's busy this year.' Klepto Joe flapped his arms wildly, trying to get Boy-o-Boy's attention, exclaiming that he was 'gasping with the thirst and can't that drunken eejit see me?'

And so it continued throughout the whole evening, with very short spells of calm that allowed everyone to draw breath for a minute before the onslaught started all over again. Finally it reached a climax around eleven that night, when the fathers, on their way home from the pubs, congregated outside the shop. Peering through the windows, while at the same time counting the money they had left over from the wages after the night's drinking, they assessed what they could afford to buy for their children (who still believed that Santa just might make it to their house that year).

By midnight, with the bells of St Michael's Church announcing the arrival of Christmas Day, the flurry had died down to the odd few drunks making their way home. All of the 'helpers' were congregating in the kitchen and toasting each other for another well-run operation. I was just starting to clean up the piles of cardboard boxes that littered the floor behind the counter when a lone drunk came staggering into the shop, dressed in a dirty old coat and swaying slightly. He came over to the mother (who was tidying up the drapery section) and reached into his pocket, dragging out a handful of coins, which he carefully placed on the counter. Then he asked the mother, very politely, 'What toys can I buy for that amount?'

Thinking that the mother would sling him out with a flea in his ear, I was amazed to hear her asking him how many children had he and what were their ages? When she had extracted the information from him, she picked up an empty box from the floor and, walking down the shelves, began to fill it with an assortment of toys, before handing it over. She then guided him to the door very gently but determinedly, and pointed him in the direction of his house with the words, 'Now, make sure that you place these in the children's room before you pass out.'

As an afterthought she called him back and, rushing behind the counter, grabbed a set of gloves and ran back out to him, stuffing them into the box as a 'gift for the wife'. Whereupon he appeared to sober up noticeably and, turning to my mother, announced in almost an apologetic voice, 'I'm sorry, Mam, but she died two year ago.'

The mother and I watched him shuffle off up the street with the cardboard box clutched tightly to his chest and, as she locked up the shop doors, I noticed tears running down her face. She turned to me, wiping her cheeks, and then she picked me up in her arms and carried me into the kitchen where the 'hooley' was about to begin – and would carry on into the early hours of the morning.

However, my father had one more task for me to perform, so he took me upstairs to their bedroom and sat me down on their bed. He told me how proud he was to have a son who had reached the age of being able to assist in the business, then emptied from his pockets bundles and bundles of notes. They were creased and folded in every conceivable manner and I was given instructions to sort them into their respective denominations. Once done, I was to count the lot, hide it under the rug, and finally to creep down and whisper to him the final figure before I went to bed. Tiredness forgotten, I set to my task with renewed vigour and, after carefully unfolding, straightening and stacking all of the notes into their respective piles, I began the task of counting and storing them. I checked each pile twice and carefully noted down the total for each bundle before totting them up.

Totally amazed, I stuffed it all under the rug and, satisfied that it was safely concealed, simply tore downstairs with such excitement that I roared from the doorway: 'Dad, Dad, we took in thousands and thousands of pounds!' And stood there grinning and hopping from foot to foot with excitement.

The room was stunned into silence, broken by the sound of a glass smashing as Boy-o-Boy dropped his drink and stuttered, 'Boy, oh boy, Ron, but that's great.'

Christmas Dolls

'THE PIPES HAVE busted, the pipes have busted!' The cry first started in the schoolyard like the soft murmur of approaching rain and slowly the news was taken up in the classrooms nearest the yard. Eventually the crescendo of noise reached our room with such force that it infected us all; even I began to chant with the others, 'the pipes have busted, the pipes have busted!', although I had no idea what it meant or what would be the consequence.

It had been our first day back at Goldenbridge School after the Christmas holidays and I had gone to bed the night before with a sense of dread at having to go back to 'that awful place with them nuns'. I was in such a state of panic that not even the grandmother (with bribery in the form of sweets, money and promised trips to the local cinema) could stem my howls of anguish. Up until the previous evening, before the awful realisation had sunk in that my Christmas holiday was over, I had been engrossed in the roadworks that were taking place on our street. They had begun at Kilmainham and, over the previous months, they had been slowly marching up the road in checkerboard slabs of concrete.

The Dublin Corporation was continuing its effort to rid Dublin of all its old tramlines and cobblestone streets. Since Emmett Road was the main exit route out of the city for all the country people returning to Cork and the southern regions, our road was enjoying the full might of the entire available workforce in an attempt to complete the works quickly.

All through that first week in January I had watched the workers from my bedroom window, which offered a panoramic view of the operation. They first cordoned off one side of the street, then the other, while they tore up the old, redundant tramlines and, using pneumatic drills, dislodged the tightly locked and deeply imbedded cobblestones, before installing large mats of steel mesh and filling the void with concrete. Throughout the day the street was filled with an unholy row from the constant jackhammering that reverberated from building to building. Whenever one crew stopped, another was already tapping out its ear-shattering response as if they were in constant communication and were trying to outdo each other.

I saw the removal of the tramlines as the end of an era, since the tracks I viewed from my bedroom window had always guaranteed amusement on a wet day. Inevitably some poor fellow cycling down the hill from Ward's pub would end up with the wheels of his bike slipping into the tramlines. Depending on his cycling ability, he would display antics worthy of a circus act in attempting to keep his balance, while avoiding being swept round the corner into Spa Road. Sometimes, of course, people just promptly fell off as soon as the wheels hit the lines. But thankfully the odd one had the skill needed to travel the whole road, with bike and body gyrating wildly from side to side, in an attempt to counteract each movement. Displaying great skill, they were able to hop the bike out of the lines before they were forced to navigate the sharp bend into the CIE compound.

Every evening the perimeter of each newly completed concrete section was secured with forty 4-gallon barrels, topped with long planks from which hessian blankets were hung. This was an attempt to keep out the stray animals that appeared to show as much interest as I did, if not more, in the freshly laid concrete. In the evening the truck arrived to collect the workforce, having first unloaded the night-watchman, complete with his galvanised, domed hut, oil-lamps, and coal brazier. With calls of 'Jimmy, don't catch your death of cold' from the departing workers, the watchman immediately set about building his coal and slack fire in the brazier. Once it was lit, he would sit close by the heat, hunched over with his head cupped in the palms of his hands, staring into the flames as if in search of the answer to some question he had spent his entire life investigating. His concentration was spasmodically interrupted by passers-by, who would engage him, briefly, in conversation, as an excuse to warm themselves by his fire. After heating their hands over the coals, they emphasised the cold of the night with the stamping of their feet on the ground and eventually, exhausting all conversation, reluctantly they moved off, allowing the watchman to return to his invisible world.

On that last night of freedom, having accepted the realisation that there was no escape from the impending doom of a new school term on the morrow, I recall being led to my bed by the grandmother. Casting a last glance at the watchman, whose face had now taken on an orange glow from over-exposure to the heat of the fire, I recall thinking that I wished I were he.

I turned and twisted in my bed, unable to sleep because the fear had settled deep in the centre of my stomach, and I listened to the quiet snores of my grandmother. The silence of the street outside was broken only by the sound of a car or bus negotiating the roadwork barriers. Or the shouts of the night-watchman directed at some dog attempting to leave his paw marks in the wet concrete, as proof of his existence on this planet: 'Geerron outa there you shaggy mongrel, geeerron, geerron before I take my stick to you.'

'The pipes have busted, the pipes have busted!' The whole school was now in uproar, with the nuns running around trying to restore order. I stood in the middle of the room with the older kids from the other classes rushing by me to the door, screaming 'no more school, no more school', before they disappeared off down the street. I still did not fully understand the problem, but was beginning to realise that, whatever had happened, it meant that we were being sent home for the duration. For me it was like a stay of execution and, with a feeling of exhilaration, I turned and collided head-on with Sister Ann. The fear of committing a sin of this magnitude caused me nearly to die with fright but, as she was so preoccupied with the problem of the burst pipes, she sent me on my way with an almost half-hearted clip over the ear. With the front door wide open and beckoning like the pathway to heaven, I joined my fellow classmates, skipping and jumping down the street towards temporary freedom. My mother was surprised to see me back home so early and we had to wait until the father arrived that evening for him to explain the 'busted pipes' story that I had repeated to her throughout the day. In his words, 'the nuns were too bloody mean to leave the heating on low throughout the holidays. So when they started it up again, all of the pipes, being frozen, just flew off the walls. If those bloody twisters spent less time praying and more time running a school, well, the lad would be back in school tomorrow.'

'Ron, not in front of the child,' admonished the mother.

That night I even said my prayers before going to bed, after taking a last look out of the window at the night-watchman who seemed to have aged more since the previous night. I jumped into bed, glad that my wish of becoming him had not come true after all, and within seconds I was fast asleep.

The next morning I woke early, as if in premonition of some great change overnight. Opening my eyes, the first thing I noticed was that the room was bathed in an eerie, pale light, and all sounds from outside were muffled as though they came from behind a wrapping of cotton-wool. I flung myself out of bed and rushed over to the window to peer out in awe at a world turned white.

Dressing as quickly as I could, I rushed downstairs and out on the street, where I began to scoop up handfuls of snow and make piles of snowballs. These I attempted to lob onto the roofs on the opposite side of the road. When I'd seen this in my comic books the snowballs had gained dramatically in size from the snow on the roofs until, gigantic in proportion, they had hurtled back down to the street.

All I succeeded in accomplishing was to incur the wrath of Mrs Malloy, whom I woke with the sound of my snowballs crashing against her bedroom window. With numbed fingers and hands, I continued throughout the day to construct snowman after snowman, until the backyard was packed with strange snow-beings in various shapes and sizes, from blobs to odd, egg-shaped mounds. But with the assistance of the father we finally produced something resembling a snowman as depicted in the *Beano*. After we had finished the masterpiece, the mother completed the sculpture with a few buttons off an old duffel coat, a scarf donated by the grandmother and one of her father's old broken pipes that he had left on his last visit.

∽

A week later I was back in Goldenbridge School with the

heating pipes repaired and the nuns lecturing us on the cost they had incurred in ensuring our comfort. Our first Holy Communion was now only a few short months away and they were intent on redoubling their efforts to teach the catechism. Eventually the big day arrived. I was up at the crack of dawn preparing for the event, beginning with a bath presided over by the grandmother. She insisted on scrubbing the back of my neck until it turned red and it felt as if she had removed the first layer of my skin. She then targeted my ears and, after cleaning them to her satisfaction, left me to complete the bathing on condition that I was to give 'down there' a good scrubbing.

Once dried, I was taken downstairs to the kitchen and stood on top of the kitchen table, wearing nothing more than a pair of white underpants. With this, both the mother and grandmother set about me, as if preparing a pedigree animal for a dog show. First the mother tried to get the black shorts on me by issuing instructions to lift first one leg and then the other. Unfortunately this coincided with an instruction from the grandmother to raise my arms so that she could attach the shirt to my carcass. Before long I was balancing on top of the table like Boy-o-Boy attempting to navigate our hallway on one of his bad nights.

When I was dressed to their satisfaction there followed a tour of the various shops. I felt like a right idiot. First I was over to Mrs Malloy, who said that my socks didn't go with the shoes. That made the mother spin me out of the place before my feet could change direction and haul me back across the street to Mrs Finnegan. She was too busy getting her daughter Ann ready for her first Holy Communion to make a fuss of me. But with that, the mother was caught with having to remark on how well Ann looked, defeating the whole purpose of showing me off in the first place. She had to settle for a bunch of women shopping in Finnegan's, who commented on how well the 'little angel' looked, '. . . and Jaysus, would you just look at the cut of him, shure, once the bishop sets eyes on him, they'll pop out of his fat head, ha, ha, ha. And Mrs Finnegan – that fish you sold me last Friday made my husband shit all night and I didn't get a wink of sleep with him coming and going.'

At the appointed hour I was led up the street towards St Michael's Church and, as I looked around me, it was as if something other-worldly was taking place. It appeared that a host of angels were descending on the church from every direction, with all the little girls attired in their white, beautiful dresses, complete with white veils of every length and description. Most of the boys were dressed similarly to me: black shorts, white shirt and tie, dark jacket or blazer. Owing to our darker dress we helped to highlight the girls' outfits. But there were the odd few exceptions. Some of the girls (although they still resembled little angels) wore off-coloured and oversized white dresses, black or brown shoes and socks of different sizes and colours. Their whole outfit screamed of something 'not quite right', and as soon as the nuns spotted them, they were discreetly directed to the side aisles.

The nuns were guarding the church entrance with an intensity that would have made the commander of an army barracks proud. As every family appeared, the child was whisked away, sorted by dress and parenthood, and ushered from nun to nun along the main aisle of the church as if he or she was the baton in a relay race. The Reverend Mother conducted the operation with hand signals (viewed from the rear, she looked like a penguin, clapping her flippers for food), with the girls being directed to the left and the boys to the right. One particular boy from my class, who was easily identified by his mop of red hair that never appeared to have seen a brush, turned up alone. He was wearing his normal school dress of odd socks, busted shoes, torn shorts and stained jumper, complete with a variety of holes of different sizes.

As the mother and I entered the church grounds, we were just in time to witness the arrival of the red-haired fellow, who had entered from the opposite gate. As soon as the three nuns at the entrance set eyes on him, they jumped in union, as if they had been shot. With cries of 'Jesus, Mary and Joseph, Sister Assumpta, would you just look at the state of him?' two of them rushed to head him off, while the other one flew inside to find the Reverend Mother. She must have given a good account of the boy's appearance, for the Reverend Mother came out of the main door, doing at least 20 miles an hour, with another group of nuns being sucked along in her wake. She skidded to a halt in front of the boy, who was looking up at the nuns with a face that proclaimed, 'What have I done wrong? I have only come to make my first Holy Communion.'

A confab began amongst the nuns, who resembled a flock of wild geese fighting over one of their young, with the Reverend Mother glaring at Sister Charlotte as if it was all her fault. She was now standing behind the boy with her two hands resting on his shoulders in a protective fashion. Suddenly, a large black car containing the bishop glided to a halt at the church entrance. Since the Reverend Mother had her back to the gate, her only warning was when the nuns facing her threw themselves to their knees whilst blessing themselves, with a speed that would have matched the movements of the tic-tac men at the race track. Turning quickly, the colour of her face now matching the white surround of her habit, she hissed instructions to the others to 'whip him inside before the bishop set eyes on him', while she shot off to catch up to the lines of priests forming beside the bishop's car.

With a jolt that nearly ripped my arm from my shoulder, I was also dragged inside and sent on my way down the aisle with a hefty shove in the back by one of the nuns. Red Head had also been bundled down the far aisle nearest the wall by two nuns who sandwiched him between them on a pew. I watch, fascinated, as he sat, stood and knelt at the nuns' prompting. All the while, he turned and looked around with such excitement on his face, as if this was the most important moment of his life. Even though he had no parent watching, he displayed a sense of pride that challenged anybody to say that he had no business there, dressed as he was.

With the organ and choir giving a rendition of the 'Ave Maria', the mass slowly marched its way towards the highlight of the day. Then, to the ringing of altar bells and incense wafted at us by priests waving silver holders on gold chains, the bishop uttered his final 'Amen' and turned to the tabernacle, withdrawing the chalice containing the 'body and blood' of Christ.

The choir once again broke into a rousing hymn and, at a clap of the Reverend Mother's hands, we all rose as one and started to file out from the pews in two columns. Girls to the left and boys to the right, we made our way up towards the long rail in front of the altar. Seconds before the first in the line reached the altar rail Red Head was rushed up to the furthest corner of the altar by his 'minders'. The two nuns knelt on either side and squashed him in the middle as if they were trying to disguise their charge. One of the priests in attendance to the bishop reached into the chalice and withdrew a single piece of communion wafer, then rushed over and quickly attached the wafer to a tongue that was poked out as far as Red Head could possibly stick it. No sooner had the priest withdrawn his hand than up jumped the nuns and, grabbing Red Head, they herded him up the aisle and out of the church by a side door.

∞

It was expected that when you finished your schooling at the Goldenbridge Convent you went across to the other side of Keogh Square and continued your education with the Christian Brothers. The very thought of this filled us all with dread, as the stories that had filtered back from the last lot of kids who had made 'The Walk' exceeded the horror of our wildest imaginings. They told of an institution that operated on beatings and stern men of God who believed that the only way to teach a child was to hammer knowledge into him.

Thankfully my mother was not going to subject me to that indignation. So it was with great relief that, a few weeks after I had made my communion, I heard I was to don my best, because we were off to Leeson Street for an interview with the principle of a private school called the Catholic University School (better known as CUS). And, 'for God's sake, don't open your mouth unless you are spoken to'. We were chauffeured by the father, who declined the invitation to join us 'as I won't be able to get a word in edgeways anyway . . . and isn't there a pub down the street where I can wait?'

The mother and I knocked on a large Georgian door halfway up Leeson Street, although it seemed totally unlikely that it could have a whole school hiding behind it. A priest, who was all smiles and kindness, duly admitted us into a waiting-room and asked us to take a seat while he went to inform the principal that we were there. At the precise moment when we were finally escorted into the principal's study, my bladder screamed 'full' to my brain. This cast a complete haze over our tour of the school and its facilities as I was too preoccupied trying to keep my legs crossed and not wet myself. However, some part of their conversation must have filtered through because, at one stage, I heard the principal remark, 'What a large gap your son has between his front teeth, Mrs Heaps.'

'Oh,' drooled the mother, while grabbing my head as if it were a large cauliflower and cranking it skywards (very nearly the final straw for my distressed bladder), 'his grandmother claims it's the sign of being a great singer, you know.'

'Well, we must have him in our school choir then.' A promise that held as much excitement for me as being told I was to be enrolled in a knitting group. But it had the mother beaming with pride. Since I was under strict instructions to be 'seen and not heard', it wasn't until we finally reached the schoolyard that, out of sheer desperation, I broke my vow of silence with 'Jaysus mister, is there a jax anywhere around here? I'm busting.'

Galloping off in the direction of the sternly pointed finger, I left the two of them in a state of shock, since I don't believe that my first words were quite in keeping with the mother's previous account of my character. It's amazing how simple things in life can affect your future. As I came out of the toilet (expecting a rebuke from the mother for my unauthorised departure) I found that a second priest had joined them. He had spotted me dashing across the yard and was so impressed with my speed and agility that, during my absence, he had enrolled me into the school's junior rugby team. I couldn't help wondering how, simply as a result of having a gap between my front teeth and needing to go to the toilet, I had ended up in the school's choir and on its rugby team in such a short time, even before starting at the school. I could only bless my lucky stars that I hadn't also thrown a few skips into my run or I might have ended up in the dance class as well.

It was our last day at Goldenbridge Convent and a gloomy silence had descended over the class, aggravated further by Sister Charlotte's quiet depression, with which she had infected the whole class. She had even forgotten to say the usual morning prayers and spent her time pacing up and down the aisle between the desks. She paused, now and again, to pat a boy over the head while peering anxiously at the door. At around eleven the silence was broken suddenly by the sound of three loud knocks on the classroom door, which caused Sister Charlotte to rouse herself into action, clapping her hands and rushing to open the door.

Simultaneously a low murmur broke out and rose rapidly to the level that can only be reached by over forty kids talking at once. It stopped just as suddenly as it had started when she threw open the door. There, standing on the threshold, were three black-coated angels of death, the height of the tallest emphasised by his thin frame and gaunt features. The light streaming through the doorway silhouetted his figure. His face, with its deep, sunken eyes, resembled a skull across which old skin had been stretched. He detached himself from the others and strode into the room, casting cold eyes on the assembly as if he was viewing a fish stall on Moore Street. As his eyes swept over each desk, he instilled such an aura of fear in us that each boy hunched down his head and took great interest in the inkwells.

The Christian Brothers had arrived to collect their charges and march them across the square, as a sort of introductory lesson, so that when they started in September they would know where to go and to what classroom they should present themselves. Even though I knew I wasn't making that walk, I sat there cowering with the rest. But not quite as much as the other poor souls, because curiosity was beginning to override my fear. With the tall one now marching up and down every aisle, examining each child intensely, I followed his movements with mounting interest. Sensing my gaze on him, he whipped his head around and glared at me with those dreadful eyes that said, 'Wait until I get you across the street, boy.' Then, with one last sneer in my direction, he stomped to the head of the class.

With a high-pitched voice and a lisp that bordered on a speech impediment he said, 'All those pupilsss thwat are going to the Qwristian Bwothers swand now.'

I barked out a laugh that I could only attribute to release of tension, causing him to glare at me with an expression that shouted 'you are dead, boy'.

All of the class stood up, bar five others and myself, and, still staring at me as if I was hard of hearing, the Christian Brother repeated the question. His look of sheer disappointment when he finally realised that he was not going to get his hands on my body gave way to an explosion of rage directed at the others. Ordering them to move out into the aisles and to stand to attention, he beckoned to his two similarly attired henchmen, who had not moved from the door as if they were expecting an escape attempt. With military precision, arms swinging, they marched the boys out of the classroom and off down the street. He slammed the door with a final glance in my direction, his features once again silhouetted by the bright light from outside, only this time he looked more comical than frightening.

Sister Charlotte had not moved once during the whole episode, nor had Skull Head made any attempt to converse with her, almost as if he believed the nuns had only been playing with our education and that they, the Brothers, were now going to show these kids what real teaching was all about. She turned to the six of us scattered around the now very empty classroom and, with a voice like that of a mother whose children have all been abducted, whispered that we were free to go. Very slowly we filed past her and went out the door and, as I was the last to leave, I turned to close it.

My last memory of that classroom, in which I received my first few years of education, was that of a nun standing in the middle of an empty, gloomy space, softly crying. The feeling of sadness lasted about three paces from the door, until the realisation of freedom and the thought of never-ending summer holidays ahead lifted my spirits. I bolted off down the street with a skip and a hop and was just in time to see, off to my right, a long line of small boys slowly marching their way across the square.

Two days later I was standing in the kitchen with my mother and grandmother who (for once) were conversing with each other, when, with a cry, the mother clutched her stomach, which appeared to have grown a lot larger over the past number of weeks. The mother grabbed the grandmother, who helped her into a chair, and instructed me to run to the dispensary and get my father as quickly as I could. By the time I returned, the mother was in the hallway with a packed bag and a blue blanket under her right arm. As the questions tumbled out of my mouth, the father led the mother to the car and settled her in the back seat. Then they drove off together in the direction of Kilmainham. When the father came back, all of the questions I had stored up dissolved quickly at his suggestion that I go with him to Newlands Golf Club and caddy for him.

The father had joined the club about ten minutes after he had bought the car and I loved these visits to the golf club, as I was allowed to play with the flags on the greens. I became the flag-holder for the seventh cavalry and could gallop up and down the fairways, leading an imaginary charge against fearsome foe. That particular evening, when we had completed the eighteen holes and a lengthy stay in the clubhouse bar, he suggested that we visit Wong's restaurant on the way home, which had me rushing to the car before he had finished talking. Wong's coleslaw was the tastiest food that I had ever eaten and, if served with a burger (another new item that I never got at home), well, I was in seventh heaven.

We arrived home as the bells of St Michael's were tolling out the midnight hour. He parked the car on the pavement outside the shop and, much to my amazement, Mrs Clooney appeared as if by magic and announced to the father that he had a baby daughter. Whereupon he turned to me, grinning like an idiot, and suggested we should visit the mother. We set off for St James's Hospital, where we found on our arrival that children were not allowed in at that time of night. Following directions from the father, I crept along the outside of the building, peering into each ground-floor room, until I could see the father standing by the mother's bedside. He opened the window when I tapped on it and helped me climb in. There, lying in a cot, wrapped in pink blankets and wearing a white bonnet, was my new sister, whom they had decided to call Catherine.

Before I could come to terms with the full delight of having a sister to look after, the door swung open – there was just enough time to duck under the high hospital bed and take cover. I watched grey-stockinged legs walk over to the bed and held my breath for fear of discovery. When the nurse had completed her ministrations (during which the mother informed her that she was not to forget that she was once a nurse too), she walked over and closed the window. She then bundled my father out of the room, telling him, 'You should know better than visit your wife at gone midnight, she needs her rest, and anyway, where were you during the birth?'

With the door closed on the two of them, I popped out from under the bed and came face to face with the mother, who was now falling asleep. Panic rose in me, since I wasn't tall enough to open the window latch. But the father returned, muttering, 'Who the hell does she think she is . . . wait until I find the matron', and once again I climbed through the window and escaped back to the car.

A week after Catherine was brought home, I was told by the father that the grandmother and I were to spend my summer holidays in Carrick-on-Suir with her other sisters on Aunt Josie's farm. While I realised that, for me, this was a real holiday, grandmother was actually being exiled back to her roots, as a result of an accident that had happened a few nights before.

It had been late evening and the grandmother and I had been in bed. Since hers was furthest from the door I witnessed her attempt to reach the toilet in time. But all she succeeded in doing was spreading a trail of diarrhoea from her bed across the floor, through the hallway and into the toilet; worse, the mother spotted this before the grandmother even had a chance to begin cleaning up. She started screaming at the grandmother and insisted that she returned to her bed. When the mother discovered that this was also destroyed, it drove her even deeper into frenzy and she demanded that the father phone his brother Stan.

Silently we all waited until we heard Stan and his wife, Mona, arrive, whereupon the mother brought them up to the bedroom. The grandmother, cowering like a disobedient child, was further subjected to the indignation of having to lie there while the mother threw back the sheets, screeching, 'Look what I have to put up with, who is going to clean up this mess? That woman has to go.'

So that is how Stan, the father, the grandmother and I

arrived at Auntie Josie's farm on a lovely summer's evening. The two brothers stayed overnight before roaring off in a cloud of dust the following morning, no doubt on a slow pub-crawl back to Dublin.

For me it was akin to being launched into the cast of Cinderella, except there was no Cinderella and the ugly sisters numbered three. Since they were all about the same age, reuniting the grandmother with her two siblings, Bridie and Josie, had the same effect as introducing a cantankerous old hen into a well-established chicken coup with a clearly defined pecking order. It was bedlam for the first week while the three of them tried to assert authority over each other. As each bedroom led off the kitchen, this area became the main battleground, allowing them a line of retreat back to their individual 'roosts' when they tired of snapping at each other. For me, it was a time of keeping out of their way and being left to my own devices that I used to full advantage, spending days exploring the countryside and assuming the roles of my heroes, from Robin Hood to John Wayne (and everybody in-between).

My seventh birthday came and went and we were galloping towards another Christmas in the shop. This Christmas Eve saw the usual bunch of misfits, with Boy-o-Boy a bit drunker that normal (if that was possible) but I was allowed to help with the parcel wrapping. During the day there was the normal flurry of shoppers, until around five in the evening one incident persuaded the father that we were entering a new era of toy buying. A fight had broken out between two men over a doll, which frightened Klepto Joe (in his usual place in the middle of the shop floor) so much that he bolted across to the Workman's Club for a 'quick stiffener'. Boy-o-Boy retreated to the drink cupboard, leaving the father to step in and break up the fracas.

Up until that particular year our stock of toys hadn't changed or varied greatly from year to year. However, this Christmas, on one of our last-minute buying trips, the father had succumbed to a dozen of the new Barbie dolls stocked by Hector Grey's – rather reluctantly, since he thought that Hector was trying his usual stunt of offloading stock that he couldn't sell easily.

'Ron, these dolls have just arrived and will be the hottest item of the year. Look, as you are one of my most valued customers, I'm giving you first pick of the litter as every little girl in Christendom will be looking for one of these from Santa this year.' The father just stood looking at him, with his arms folded and eyebrows raised, while Hector continued getting more excited by the minute.

'Christ, man, where have you been for the past week? Have you not heard all the advertisements for them? My shipment only arrived this afternoon. Christ, man, I'm giving you gold.' Once the father heard the words 'most valued customer' and 'I'm giving you gold', he was even more convinced that Hector was trying to offload useless stock on him.

Nothing Hector could say could convince him otherwise, but he agreed to purchase a dozen anyway. When we arrived home and placed one of the Barbie dolls on display in the window, the stock of dolls barely lasted fifteen minutes and was the cause of the row between the two men who were arguing over who had seen the last doll first.

Never one for leaving an opportunity pass him by, the father instructed the mother to place a large sign in the front window announcing that we would have Barbie dolls for sale again later that evening. He grabbed me and, before I knew it, the pair of us were in the old Popular racing back to Liffey Street, the car shuddering and vibrating violently as if we were driving on the tyre rims only. All the while he was driving, he was talking to himself in an attempt to come up with a plausible excuse as to why we had reappeared in Hector's shop after only a few short hours. How was he going to get his hands on Hector's stock of dolls without having to pay through the nose for them?

Skidding to a halt outside the wholesalers, the father was out of the car and in the door before the engine had stopped, relief washing over him because the place was still open. He composed himself and wandered over to the drink table, where Hector was telling a story to a group of buyers in no hurry home. Spotting the father, he cut short what he was saying and roared out to him, 'I told you I was giving you gold and there was you thinking that this Jew boy was trying to sell you a pig in a poke. When has old Hector ever let you down?' And he poured the father a whiskey, while winking to the others.

'Dolls? What dolls?' said the father in mock surprise. 'Oh the Barbies, Christ, I haven't even unloaded them from the car yet, they're still in the boot. No Hector, I came back for a gross of caps for the toy guns . . . eerr, son, will you grab a gross of the red caps from one of the lads and load them into the car? Speaking of dolls, Hector, just out of curiosity, do you have any left?'

'Dolls, dolls,' Hector reflected, as his hands swept in an arc towards the general direction of his shelves. 'I've got millions of dolls. I've got Chinese, Taiwanese and Japanese, little ones and big ones, I've even got a doll that you could take to bed with you.' Which caused the gang around the table to howl with laughter.

The father, realising that he was beaten and time was ticking away, capitulated: 'All right Hector, you were right about the bloody Barbie dolls, they went like hot cakes, how many do you have left?'

'About nine dozen, give or take a few, and, as it's Christmas, they're still at the old price.'

'I'll take the lot,' says the father, 'Right boys, quickly, load them up, I have to get back before the punters break up the shop.' He explained about the row breaking out over the last doll in the shop, while Hector's minions loaded the car.

No matter how hard he tried we couldn't get them all into the car and, as two trips were out of the question, it ended with the father driving me and two large cardboard boxes of dolls over to Dame Street. He deposited the dolls and me on a 21 bus, and then returned to Hector's to collect the remainder in the car. The bus conductor, none too kindly, was helping me off with my two large boxes at the Emmett Road stop when the father arrived, just in time to receive the full force of the conductor's displeasure.

'Jaysus, Mister, do these boxes and kid belong to you?'

'And a Happy Christmas to you, my good man.'

'I'm bleeden' well not your "good man" and what the feck do you think CIE is anyway, a bleeden' freight company? Next time I'll bleeden' well throw them off.'

'And a Happy Christmas to all of your family.' The father completely ignored the irate bus conductor and said to me, 'Now quick, Son. Let's get them in the car, we'll have to bring them in through the hall door, the shop is mobbed.'

I couldn't believe the amount of people surrounding the front of the shop. Apparently they had come from miles around when news had travelled that we still had Barbie dolls for sale; it was bedlam. The father unloaded the first batch into our hallway, leaving Boy-o-Boy in charge of moving the stock from the hall into the back of the shop, where eager customers were waiting with money in hand to grab their prize. Boy-o-Boy decided to take a look for himself at what all the excitement was about. Swaying slightly, with boxes scattered around his feet, he had just removed a doll from its box and was peering under its dress when he caught sight of the father. Holding a glass of whiskey in one hand and waving the doll above his head like a baton in the other, he cried, 'Boy, oh boy, look Ron, she's even got a little pair of knickers on! What will they think of next, miniature bras no doubt?'

Looking in through the open shop doors, all I could see was a press of people shoving and pushing each other in an attempt to get close to the counter, while those who had already been served were trying to squeeze their way back out. All of a sudden, like a cork popping out of a bottle, Klepto Joe came catapulting out through the double doors, with arms flapping wildly and his clothing all in disarray. Steadying himself on the pavement, he spied the father with the car boot wide open and turned to the crowd in the shop, roaring at the top of his voice, 'Barbie dolls here. Come, get your Barbie doll from the man with the car.' Whereupon he turned on his heels and, for the second time that evening, fled across the road to the Workman's Club.

Whatever Joe's intention had been in informing the masses, it certainly relieved the pressure inside the shop. All the father had to do was to flog the dolls, unwrapped, from the back of the old Popular. Hector would have been proud of us. We resembled two hawkers on Moore Street, with the father taking the money and pointing out the person to whom I should hand over the doll. He also raised the price to round it off to a nice three quid, so that he didn't have to give any change.

All in all, that particular Christmas turned out to be a very profitable one, especially with the extra money he made from the Barbie dolls. In the early hours of Christmas morning, after I had tallied the take in their bedroom, I briefly joined in the hooley that was in full swing in the kitchen. Most of them in there were giving Klepto Joe abuse for deserting his post. Joe, of course, kept blaming Boy-o-Boy for not supplying him with any drink, while Boy-o-Boy blamed the father for having placed him briefly on Barbie doll detail.

'Boy, oh boy, Ron, I wouldn't have believed it unless I had seen it with my own eyes. Boy, oh boy, grown men chasing around Dublin after a little doll, boy, oh boy, we'll never see the like of those antics in this shop again.'

Confessions of an Alcoholic

ONE EVENING I arrived home from school to find the mother rocking to and fro in her chair, holding Catherine in her arms and crying her eyes out. After telling me repeatedly that I was too young to understand, she finally owned up that the father had admitted he was an alcoholic. And that he had signed himself into St Patrick's Hospital, just off Thomas Street on a side road that led to Kingsbridge Station.

Although not fully understanding the implications of the father confessing he was an alcoholic, I was still completely overwhelmed by the mother's distress and sorrow. Equally, we kids couldn't really comprehend how serious it was that he had drunk all of the shop's Christmas takings, but soon all three of us were bawling our eyes out and reassuring each other that everything would turn out just fine. That night Catherine was moved into my room and, before the pair of us fell asleep, we pushed our beds closer together for comfort. At some time during the night Catherine crept into my bed and the two of us snuggled up together; that was to become a nightly ritual.

Every evening Catherine stood by the hall door awaiting my arrival home from school, and as soon as she spotted me walking down the street she would shout, 'Nn, Nn's home.' Then she would rush up and throw her arms around my waist. One particular evening, after receiving a good walloping from the headmaster at school, I stomped in and pushed her out of my way, taking great delight in informing her that it would be her turn next to go to school. At this she stopped short, looked up at me, and stated firmly, 'I will never go to school.'

Later that week, after school, the mother, Catherine and I caught the 21A bus, got off at the top of Thomas Street and walked the short distance to St Patrick's to visit the father. We were directed to his private room where we all just stood around watching each other without saying a word, while the father sat on his bed wearing his suit and slippers, staring at the floor. My mother broke the silence by saying that she had met the head psychiatrist that morning.

'Ron, for the children's sake, will you admit that you are an alcoholic and give up the drink?'

'I am not an alcoholic and I don't have a drink problem.'

This change of tune puzzled me slightly.

'Then why did the doctor tell me this morning that you were and that they have you on anti-booze pills?'

'I only told him that so I could get into this place for a rest.'

'Then why did you tell him that you had a drink problem?'

It was as if the mother had pushed an imaginary button. The father jumped up from his bed and, his face contorted with rage, roared at the mother, 'So that I could fucking well get away from you, you bitch; nag, nag, nag, that's all you ever do, even your fucking children are sick of you, just ask them, you bitch.'

With that, he pushed past her and, nearly ripping the door off its hinges, stomped his way down the corridor, shouting, 'She's at me again, she's at me again.'

Catherine and I had backed away into the corner of the room, holding each other. As his shouts echoed down the wide hallway, the mother, crying, gathered us up and we headed out to catch the bus back home. Over the weekend the mother decided that I should call into him on the way home from school and try to convince him that he should give up the drink. So every evening, instead of taking the usual bus home, I would cross St Stephen's Green and walk down Grafton Street into Dame Street, where I would catch the 21 or 21A bus.

The first time I visited the father, he had returned to his old self as if the other evening's abuse had never happened. Once he had taken his time explaining to me that he did not have a drink problem, and that it was the only way that he could get some peace and rest from the mother, he brought me on a tour of the place. There was a full-sized snooker table that I could play any time I wanted and a games room, complete with a stage, where the inmates played whist of an evening. They were an odd mixture from all walks of life and included several priests and nuns.

He gave a comic account of the shock therapy he had been given. With a motion of cupping his hands around his head to simulate the band that had been attached to it, he explained how they had plugged him into a wall socket and shot electric volts through his head that had made his face twitch. And how, every morning, he palmed his pills and pretended that he was taking the anti-booze tablets. If they were watching him really closely, he could pop the pills into his mouth, hide them under his tongue, swallow the water, and, after the nurse had left the room, spit them back out again. So by the time he had finished, the father was once again the best person in the world as far as I was concerned, and my mother the biggest anti-Christ of all time.

Over the following weeks I became the peace envoy between the pair of them, passing messages back and forth, until we had all convinced ourselves that he was not really an alcoholic after all, and that all he was suffering from was overwork. We also convinced ourselves that the doctors were nothing but a bunch of shysters and, since he was a private patient, that all they were trying to do was extract as much money as they could from the health insurance company which was footing the bill.

But there was one situation I never told the mother about, since the father had sworn me to secrecy. Every evening on arrival at the hospital, instead of entering through the front doors, I crept around the side of the building. After I had tapped on a window that the father had shown me, it would be opened and I would be gazing into a room filled with people. Handing in my school bag to the father, I would be given slips of paper wrapped with money and I would dash off up the street to the corner pub. On my return, clutching in both arms large brown bags full of bottles, I would pass the lot through the window, then walk back in through the main entrance where the uniformed porter would check my school bag to see if I was carrying anything. I was always met by a hero's welcome as I strode back into the games room to accept my delivery fee. Feeling like a king and slapped on the back by all present, I was then taken off to join the inmates in a game of snooker or whist.

After a couple of weeks of this routine the father discharged himself from hospital. When I arrived home, the father and mother were laughing and joking together in the kitchen, all animosity between them gone, or at least well hidden. To celebrate his homecoming the pair of them went to the Workman's Club after Catherine and I had been put to bed. There, from the upstairs bar, they could have a drink and watch our bedroom window across the street.

The father also took that opportunity to announce to the mother that he had been elected by the local Fianna Fáil

Cumann to stand as their TD candidate in the next general election. The ensuing row lasted a week, with the mother claiming that they were only making a fool of him by their nomination. That all they wanted from him was the five-hundred-pound registration fee, which would be used to ensure that one of the other two Fianna Fáil nominees got in.

He argued that he was the Home Assistance Officer for the area, and consequently well known (especially with us having the shop), and so he would get a large percentage of the local vote. As he needed only 2,200 first preference votes to get elected, he should easily walk into the position. So it continued, arguing back and forth late into the night. The performance had Catherine and I cowering up in our beds, listening to the shouting, and hoping that neither of them would come into our room to enlist our support for their argument. I still remember the hurt on my father's face when, one evening, the mother stood me in the middle of the kitchen floor between them. She asked me to choose between her and the father, the question being reinforced with nods and smiles from her. When I ran into the mother's arms, I watched the father get up and resignedly walk out of the room.

My eighth birthday fell at the end of this period of silence and Shady Steven, along with his girlfriend, brought me out for the day. When they dropped me back at the house, I was delighted to find that the parents were once again talking. The mother announced that the father had decided not to run in the local election after all.

Looking back, I can't pass judgement on who was right or wrong. Perhaps the mother was correct in her assessment of the nomination, or maybe the father was accurate in his own appraisal that he could have 'walked' the election. What I do know is that when I saw the father standing by the sink that evening, it was as if a light had gone out in him. Instead of a tall, straight-backed man, oozing confidence, a sad, dejected person who appeared to have given up had replaced him. That Christmas Eve, with the usual hustle and bustle going on in the shop, the father spent the entire evening upstairs, dressed in his pyjamas, walking from room to room with a hot-water bottle strapped to his leg, complaining of cramp.

The following day's Christmas dinner was eaten in complete silence. Straight after Christmas the mother began taking Catherine and I for evening walks, regardless of the weather, and this is when I developed my love for being out on stormy nights, with the rain pelting off a waterproof jacket and the wind howling all around us, cocooned in warm clothes. We would walk past Goldenbridge Convent, up by the Grand Canal, cross at Bluebell, walk along the Drimnagh side, and then cross back again at the lock gates opposite Sperrin Road. All the while the mother was discussing the possibility of leaving the father, saying that she would take Catherine and me, or, if I wanted, I could stay with him. On returning home she fed us hot soup before sending us to bed, where Catherine and I lay awake discussing the implications of the mother's threat to leave the father. We agreed with each other that it was all only talk and that I would look after her, especially when she reached the age of having to go to school. Then we would slip into a troubled sleep.

Somewhere along the way we bought a brand new caravan and the father parked it up on the footpath for a week before we took it on our holidays to Tramore; it was our first family holiday together. We set off one Sunday morning, with the old Popular car straining under the pressure of having to tow this new acquisition, and headed off into the country. We got as far as the Naas Road before the car overheated and the radiator had to be topped up with water from bottles stored in the caravan. The whole trip took nearly ten hours and Catherine and I spent most of the journey either sleeping or peering out of the caravan's large back window at the long lines of traffic that built up behind us. Owing to the twists and turns of the narrow country roads, the vehicles behind us were unable to pass unless we pulled in at a town along the way for our compulsory 'engine-cooling stops'.

On our arrival at Tramore, the father discovered a section of road that had been turned into a cul-de-sac by the construction of a new road and, driving down to the end, he unhitched the caravan and jacked it into its permanent resting place. For there was no way that the car would survive another journey with it in tow.

The day before we packed up to return to Dublin, the father collected the grandmother from Carrick-on-Suir, along with her assorted possessions, and transported her back to our caravan, informing her on arrival, 'Mother, see what we have bought you, this is going to be your new home.' I have no idea what she thought of her 'new home', but she just shuffled in and began to re-arrange the interior. This radical change of plan was provoked by the situation back on the farm. Instead of life improving for the three sisters, it had deteriorated to a point where Bridie had locked herself in her room and refused to come out until 'that sister of mine dies or leaves. And it had better be quick, as I'm not feeling too well myself.'

After installing the grandmother in her caravan to face the coming winter on her own, we took off for Dublin with the grandmother waving her hanky after us. Ahead of me was a new school term, in new class, with a different teacher.

∞

I realised very early on that snobbery was something that was built into my new school's foundations, and it divided the pupils into two very separate categories: the children of parents who could afford to send their kids to the school and the kids whose parents couldn't afford to, but did anyway. I fitted into the latter minority group and, along with my companions, was constantly reminded of this fact. However, instead of making us feel inferior, it instilled us with a sense of pride, which I would voice when the occasion arose with comments such as, 'Well, at least our parents are working for their money and not ripping off the population like yours, pretending they are doctors or barristers.' Needless to say, this would sometimes result in the matter being settled down a lane on the way home from school. But mostly, since the other kids already believed that we came from 'bad neighbourhoods', they tended to avoid too much physical confrontation.

I was beginning to develop a hatred for school and an instinctive fear of the teachers. If I had been asked why, I could not have responded with any definite reason, except to say that I 'just did'. I had started third class and had been elevated up another flight of stairs. My new classroom faced into the recreation yard and, on day one, I grabbed the end desk at the back of the class over by the window. My intention was to keep a very low profile, with my head down, for I hoped to get through the year without drawing too much attention to my person. In this school we were taught by a priest and his main brief was to pound the English language into us at any cost.

Twice a day, at around eleven in the morning and three in the afternoon, the school principal visited each class to take the roll call and administer punishment to offenders. Any boy that the teachers thought deserved a 'good hiding' would be expelled from his classroom to wait in the hallway outside for the principal's arrival. And every class could judge the principal's progress down the corridor by the ferocious whacking noises as hands were belted with the short leather strap that he carried in one of the pockets of his long, black gown. The worst part of this punishment was not the physical belting, which was bad enough (after six of the best your hands would sting and burn for the rest of the day): it was the anticipation. Especially if you had been slung out late in the afternoon after the principal, nicknamed 'the Black Death', had departed. Then you had that entire evening and the next morning to contemplate your impending punishment. By the time the Black Death did arrive, it was a kind of mental release from the images that the mind had conjured up.

On the second week back after the school holidays, one morning just after ten, the principal came into our class with a new boy in tow. After introducing him to the teacher and the class in general, he looked around, spotted the empty seat alongside me, and directed the boy to sit there. During lunch hour we discovered that we had several things in common, since he lived on Moran Road, Drimnagh, which was just across the canal from Inchicore. His name was David and he told me that his father worked for CIE as a bus inspector; what with my father being a Home Assistance Officer, here was yet another thing we had in common to draw us together and distance us from the rest of the pupils. Of course, David had to go through the obligatory inquisition with the mother on his first visit to our home. He just about scraped by with his responses and we began visiting each other's houses after school on a regular basis. David had one great advantage over me, which quickly manifested itself as the school term progressed. Namely, he could read, write and, more importantly, spell much better than me. In fact, the whole class could. More and more I found myself standing outside the classroom door awaiting the arrival of the Black Death.

Every evening, as part of our homework, we were given a page from our spelling book and had to learn to spell and pronounce the list of random words off by heart. Arriving home every evening, I would first get the father to help me pronounce the words and, once remembered, endeavour to commit their spelling to memory. That book was the last thing I read before going to sleep at night and was brought back out on the bus ride into school every morning. The next day I would I sit in the classroom, with perspiration running down my back and my palms sweating, listening to the priest firing out words at the other pupils. They, in turn, leapt to their feet and rapped out the correct spelling, until inevitably, working his way randomly through the class, he would call my name. The demand, 'Heaps, spell "emancipate"', sounded like a death sentence to me.

The whole class would hold its collective breath, waiting to burst out laughing after I had made a complete balls-up of my effort. After giving me a few more words to try, all ending in the same result, he would point to the door with an expression that said, 'Dear Lord, what more can I do?' Whereupon I would get up and, to the 'tut-tuts' of the others, make the now familiar walk to take up my usual position in the corridor waiting for the Black Death's arrival.

David tried to assist me during the first week by whispering the correct spelling, but, when he was caught and had to join me outside as a result of his one-and-only personal conflict with Father Dooley, he abandoned that idea. After about six weeks of this daily entertainment at my expense, the priest finally gave up on me and we settled down, as far as spelling was concerned, to a truce whereby he simply ignored me. Just throwing the odd comment in my direction, such as, 'Think yourself lucky, as dustbin collectors don't need to be able to spell.'

It was a great pity that in those days schools didn't understand or recognise dyslexia, because if they had it might have eased the embarrassment, frustration, fear and constant ridicule I suffered until I finished my education.

Around that time the father decided that he needed a rest. Or at least that was the story issued for the sake of the neighbours, since the truth was that he had admitted himself to St Patrick's Hospital again, but this time with a vast difference. Once again the mother and I entered the long, and now familiar, corridors of the hospital. However, instead of going directly to his room on our first visit, we were diverted to see the psychiatrist who was in charge of the institution. Once we were seated in front of him, he leant forward across his desk with his arms folded and began to explain in very simple English exactly what was wrong with the father.

'Mrs Heaps, your husband is an alcoholic and has been for many years, and the most difficult part of his treatment will be getting him to admit to himself that he has a drink problem. As a family unit you must all encourage him to quit, for the sake of his children and marriage and, while he can never drink again, once cured he will be able to enjoy a normal, happy life. Now have you any questions?'

The mother hit him with a litany of what she had had to put up with over the past years and told him that if the father had not admitted himself this time, she would have left him and taken the children. 'Especially since the last "holiday" he spent in this place was better than anything you'd get in a first class hotel,' she added.

'Now, now, Mrs Heaps, you can rest assured that when he comes out of here this time he will be a new man.' Turning to me he continued, '. . . and, young man, you, particularly, must be on your guard, as he will try to convince you that he is not an alcoholic and maybe . . . ha, ha . . . be so bold as to even convince you to bring him drink.'

At that statement I went bright red, remembering the last

time, when I had not only brought booze to the father, but had probably supplied half of the hospital as well; no wonder they were all back in drying-out again. I had visions of the inmates compiling their drink orders at that very minute, having seen me arrive, and resolved that no matter what the father said or promised me I would not bring him any drink.

Concluding, he said that if the father did not kick the habit he would eventually kill himself. Then he stood up and led us off to see him. But this time, instead of going to a private ward, we went through two sets of locked double doors, which were opened by the nurse on duty in a small office between them, and finally entered a room with six other beds.

The room was in semi-darkness and, as we approached the bed, I thought that we had been directed to the wrong person. The man I was looking at could not be my father. Before me was a gaunt, sallow-faced figure, heavily sedated, unshaven, with the appearance of some wino who had been collected off the street and dumped in here to sleep it off. As I turned to move away, I suddenly noticed features about him that were familiar until, with cold terror creeping over me, I finally grasped that this man and my father were one and the same. The mother led me out of the ward down to the canteen, still in a state of shock. She sat me down and began to explain why she had been so strict with me and what she had endured over the past few years with the father.

Since the father had spoiled me from an early age, she began, by the time she realised he had a drink problem it was too late to change my view of him. She recognised that I would side with him and, if Catherine had not been born, she would have walked out on the two of us. Over the past couple of years, with his drinking going from bad to worse, her main concern had been to protect my sister and that was why she had insisted that I be sent away for every holiday.

Crying openly, she went on to tell me how almost every evening after he returned from drinking with the boys he would be 'at her'. Although not fully understanding what being 'at her' meant, I did realise that it was something she recoiled from and hated, for while she was saying the words she began to shudder. With tears streaming down her face, she continued as if talking to herself, which caused the other people seated in the room to cast reproachful glances in our direction. She told me that over the years she had looked to the church for help. One evening, after pouring her heart out in the confessional, the priest had leapt out and dragged her from the confessional box, sending her on her way with the words 'for God's sake woman, go home to your husband'.

The two of us were now crying and I began to think that I was the cause of most of the problems: if I had been a better son to both of them, well, perhaps this would never have happened. When we finally left, I cast a last glance down the corridor that led off in the direction of the father's room and I resolved that, whatever happened, I would make sure Catherine would never be subjected to this.

We were not allowed to visit him for the next six days. On day seven, when I arrived after school and was admitted into his ward through the locked doors, I was greeted by the same gaunt figure I had seen lying in the bed on the first night. His face lit up with joy at the sight of me, he grabbed me by the arm and, sitting me down on his bed, he whispered, 'Now look Em, I don't know what lies they told you about me, but you have got to believe me when I tell you that I don't have a drink problem. It's just living with that mother of yours that has me in here with all of these other lunatics. Now be a good lad and run off and sneak me in a small naggin.'

When I responded with 'No, Dad, I won't', it was as if I had hit him in the face with a baseball bat and he staggered back until he knocked against the bedside locker. Reaching for a Player's cigarette, he lit it with hands that were shaking so badly it took him nearly a minute to coordinate the timing with his vibrating lips. After exhaling a cloud of smoke, he stared at me with bloodshot eyes and said in a low voice, 'So the bitch has got to you as well.'

'No, Dad, I've been talking to the doctor and he told me that you have a drink problem and, for me and my sister's sake, you have to get better.'

'Get out, get out,' he roared, getting up from the bed and reaching out as if he was about to strike me. 'You're no son of mine, go home and tell that bitch of a mother of yours that I will die in this stinking place.'

I ran to the door, which was being opened by two nurses coming to investigate the shouting, and, pushing past them, I ran all the way home. Before entering the shop, I made up my mind to tell the mother and Catherine that he was still sedated and I had not been allowed to talk to him. Every evening after that I made excuses to the mother as to why I could not visit the father. Instead I looked after Catherine in the evenings, while she made the trip to the hospital. Finally, about three weeks after my visit, the mother announced that the three of us were going in that evening to visit him.

I was full of apprehension as we entered the canteen, but there, already seated and awaiting our arrival, was the father that we all remembered. Clean-shaven, well-dressed, clear-eyed and with a weight gain that seemed to suit him, he greeted us all as if the past few weeks had never happened. Sitting us down, he told us that, while he didn't believe he had a drink problem, for everyone's sake and to keep our mother happy, he had decided to stop drinking. In a teasing voice he added, 'And I'll attend the AA meetings after I've been discharged from this nut-house, even though it's a complete waste of time.' With Catherine bouncing on his knee and me hugging him around the neck, the mother smiling and looking years younger, he set about telling us amusing stories about the 'crackpots' and 'cranks' that he was forced to put up with in hospital.

I celebrated my ninth birthday in a room off Williams Square filled with men and women of all ages, some with and some without their families, trying to suppress the feeling of jubilation that had come over me. Finally, when it was my father's turn to speak, I watched him walk up to the top of the room and turn to address the assembly. I took my mother's hand with choking pride and a sense of release washed over me as I heard him begin his address with the words: 'Good evening ladies and gentleman, my name is Ron, this is my first visit, and I am an alcoholic.'

Two days before the father was discharged from the 'nut-house' the mother and I had another meeting with the resident psychiatrist. We found him lounging back in his large office chair and he beckoned us over with a wave of his hand, like the Pope summoning his cardinals. Without once looking in our direction, he began to address the ceiling: 'We've done very well, yes indeedey, yes indeedey.'

I couldn't tell if his reference to 'we' referred to us, the family, or his assortment of white-coated bouncers called staff. So I decided not to show any outward sign of emotion and sat on the edge of the chair with my back as straight as possible. He continued, 'But the real battle is just beginning, for when he leaves our fine establishment diligence, yes, diligence will be required if we are to continue the work that we have begun here.' He swivelled upright in his chair and swung around to face us with a speed that caused us both to recoil into our seats with surprise.

'He will, of course, remain on the anti-booze tablets for

the foreseeable future and you must ensure that he takes them every day. He must also continue to attend the AA meetings that I believe you accompanied him to? Yes, yes, encourage, encourage, is what I say.'

He tapped the table with his fingers as if to beat out a rhythmic tattoo that would make us remember his words, '. . . and hopefully we will not see him back here for treatment ever again.'

He stopped abruptly, as if suddenly unplugged, and the room was thrown into silence while he leant both of his elbows on the desk and, cupping his two palms together, trapped his nose with the index finger of both hands, as if in deep thought. When his nose began to turn bright red the mother and I glanced at each other thinking that we had lost him, that he was going into a trance – and remembered that the father had warned us that all psychiatrists were a little mad themselves. Suddenly, he bolted out of his chair as if it had unexpectedly become red-hot, strutted over to the bookcase, leant on it and continued speaking, while taking a great interest in his books, almost as though he had just noticed that he had bookshelves.

'Before he leaves here you must search your home from top to bottom, leave no stone unturned. You must check the bathroom, the car, the bedroom, even the dog if you have one. Take my word for it, these people can hide their supplies of booze anywhere, even in their pyjamas.'

That's it, I thought, the man has spent so many years trying to cure mad people that he has become one himself. Just as I was beginning to imagine calling in a brace of his white-coated bouncers to restrain and carry him off to one of his own beds, the mother thanked him for all his help in curing her husband and most especially for his advice.

As we left the hospital she explained the meaning of the

doctor's words, and the next day all of us, including Catherine, searched the house and shop from top to bottom. By the time we had completed the hunt there were over fifteen bottles of Powers whiskey, in various stages of consumption, stacked on the kitchen table. They ranged from unopened to almost empty, as if the drinker had been interrupted before he could finish the contents and had had to re-hide the bottle hastily. We found bottles in every hiding place imaginable, from the obvious to the downright ingenious. Our first probe netted four bottles only, a tally that we were quite content with until, without any rhyme or reason, I decided to check under the cistern lid of the toilet and found a full bottle bobbing about. Which meant that we had to begin all over again, only this time searching the most extreme and unusual locations.

We found them jammed under the clear-out tray of the gas cooker, at the bottom of his golf bag between the clubs, under the mattress of Catherine's bed, attached to a string hanging in the linen cupboard, and out in the shed balancing on the roof rafters. The most obvious and therefore, to my mind, the most ingenious, was a previous Christmas present of a bottle of whiskey that the father had left on one of the shelves by the fireplace, apparently un-opened. Still in its 'Merry Christmas' gift wrapping, it seemed to suggest that we leave it untouched as, of course, father was not drinking whiskey any more, sticking only to the beer. On closer examination the wrapping paper had clearly been carefully rewrapped, the bottle was half-empty – in fact we concluded that he had continually replaced each bottle, when empty, under our very noses.

Staring at our tally, totally stunned, the mother estimated the monetary value of the bottles we had stacked in front of us – and I realised how dire the consequences would have been for the family if the father had not gone in to dry out. And, yes, I finally appreciated the anxiety the mother must have lived with over the past number of years. I knew suddenly that whatever she had told me over those years I would have sided with the father, since I had always believed he was the injured party; and I left that table with feelings of guilt, confusion and a sense of betrayal and loss.

Betrayal by the father who had lied to me for years, claiming that he didn't have a drink problem. Betrayal by the mother, because she didn't have the courage to leave him, taking Catherine and me with her so that we were away from the constant rows and arguments. I had a sickening fear of the future and what it might hold, for I didn't believe that the parents could forget all that had happened between them and live a normal life again. But, for now, all I could do was wait and see, and ensure that I protected my sister to the best of my ability.

∞

The same day the father was discharged from the 'nut-house', I met Naty, who had moved in across the street. He was two or three years older than me but, since he couldn't find any company of his own age, he decided to put up with me. Having no intention of lowering himself to my age level, he set about elevating me to his. His first introductory lesson was on the proper or, as it turned out, improper use of fireworks. I stared in wonder at the sight of the six bangers, stored in their long cigarette-type box, with their Chinese writing that probably said, 'Danger! Keep out of the reach of children': they were totally illegal in Ireland. As I watched in awe, he lit one and tossed it a good 30 feet, where it exploded with a loud bang, which had Mrs Malloy rushing out to her backyard and shouting at Naty over the wall.

'Stop using them bangers or I'll put the Inspector on you when he gets home and who is that boy with you? Is that young Heaps? You go home this minute or I'll tell your mother.'

Agreeing to meet up over the weekend, as there was no way I would be allowed out during the week, I ran home with anticipation of fun to come.

'Hey Missus, got any bangers?' As instructed by Naty, I had gone to Moore Street after school the next day and approached a rather large lady who was attending her stall and calling out at the top of her voice, 'Ripe tomatoes, a shilling a pound.'

Peering at me after I had asked her my question, she pointed me over to a woman selling bananas a little further on, who was even bigger than she was.

'Hey Missus, got any bangers?'

After glancing up and down the street, the banana-lady whispered, 'Two-and-six, sonny, a shilling for the squibs, and if you want rockets I'll have them tomorrow.'

I handed over the half-crown and she dived down the front of her dress, exposing a pair of the most enormous breasts that I had ever seen. She rooted around for a few seconds, with me blushing bright red at the sight, then extracted a box of bangers from her inner cleavage. I stored them quickly in my school bag and raced out of the street, expecting to get arrested at any moment.

There was not a lot for a nine- and a twelve-year-old to do on Emmett Road in the evenings, unless you were prepared to make your own entertainment. Armed with two packets of bangers, that is exactly what we set out to do. First we went down to the Black Lion pub, where we proceeded to clear the Saturday night revellers from the bar, which was packed to capacity. We hid in the recess of the entrance, with me keeping guard to ensure no late arrivals disturbed us. Naty took out the five bangers left in his box and, lighting the fuses, opened

the door just enough to allow his hand through, then scattered
the 6-inch, smouldering tubes across the floor. They created
absolute mayhem within seconds and we had just enough time
to dash across the street, take up refuge in the confines of a
darkened shop doorway, and watch the entertainment. In
quick succession the five bangers went off with ear-splitting
cracks – and almost simultaneously the doors of the pub were
flung back, nearly tearing them off their hinges. Confusion
reigned as the rush of drinkers tried to escape the hullabaloo
and smoke, with the racket compounded by the sound of
breaking glasses. Bewildered, the first of the refugees hit the
street.

'Jaysus Christ, what the fuck happened?'

'No bleeden' idea, but one of them things landed on me
fucking foot and I booted it into the bleeden' air.'

'So you're the fucker who caused it to go off right into me
ear! I'll be bleeden' well deaf for weeks, you big bollox.'

'Is it the bleeden' Germans again?' This came from an old
fellow who had staggered out, still holding on to his pint.

'No Dad, it's not the bleeden' Germans again, just a
bunch of kids who I'll bleeden' well kill if I ever catch them.'
Turning to another he said, 'That's all he ever talks about, the
bleeden' Germans. He was over at the Five Lamps during the
Emergency when the Germans bombed the place, and every
time he hears a loud noise he shits himself.'

With the pavement filled to overflowing, two white-
shirted barmen rushed out and scanned the street, ready to
bolt after any fleeing figures they could spot. Still glancing up
and down the road, they herded the drinkers back in to the bar
with the words, 'It's ok, it's ok, it was only kids messing and if
they ever try that again, the little bollixes, we'll kick their arses
up and down the street.'

As the road returned to tranquillity, the pair of us, still

well hidden in the shadows, were holding our sides with pent-up laughter. I was just about to move off when Naty dragged me back down. At that moment the pub door flew open with a crash and the two barmen rushed out and scrutinised the empty street again, until satisfied that the culprits had long gone. They shrugged their shoulders at each other and finally went back in, allowing us to make our way home.

Over the coming months we became the terror of the street with our banger escapades and, realising the desperate consequences if we were ever caught, we decided never to attack the same place twice running. Because Naty's father was a regular there, the Black Lion pub was ruled out as a future possibility, which made me breathe a sigh of relief. Relief, because after the euphoria of that night's events had worn off, it had been replaced by the fear of how close we had come to having the crap beaten out of us. The Workman's Club and the buses became our main targets, and we alternated between the two each weekend. At the rear of the Club the gents' toilets had been constructed adjacent to an alleyway and, by climbing out along the steel waste pipes that ran the length of the building, we could peer in through the windows directly overlooking the three cubicles. There we waited, completely hidden in the darkness, until some poor, unsuspecting drunk entered and pulled down his trousers. Once he was settled on his business, we would lob a couple of bangers into his lap, which caused a variety of different responses. Most of them came crashing out of the toilets with their trousers down around their ankles, deafened by the noise of the explosion that the tiled walls magnified tenfold. And demanding to know from all in the bar, 'What the fuck was the place coming to when a worker couldn't even take a shit in peace?'

One poor fellow was so shocked by the sight of two bangers landing on the ground at his feet that he remained riveted to the toilet seat, reciting the 'Hail Mary' over and over. After they exploded, he farted so long and loud that we nearly fell off the pipes with laughter.

The buses proved harder nuts to crack, as the challenge lay in how to get a projectile into the bus without getting caught. We began by standing at the bus stop and, when the bus pulled away after collecting its passengers, we tried to lob a couple of lit bangers into the downstairs section. On our first attempt a diligent conductor quickly hit the bell to stop the bus and, to our amazement, jumped off and chased us up the street. Overtaking Naty, he smacked him over the ears so hard that his head hurt for a week. In later months we perfected our method to cause a little more devilment. Now only one of us (usually me, as I was the faster runner) would chuck the banger inside, aiming it to land at the conductor's feet. The conductor would hit the bell, stop the bus, leap off and try to catch me. Naty, who was standing in the shadows minding his own business, would calmly step onto the platform and, with two sharp taps on the bell, send the bus on its way without its conductor. The conductor might be a hundred yards up the road before he realised that he had just lost his bus. Eventually a passenger would inform the driver that the bus was missing one of its most important components if CIE ever wanted to make money. So the driver, bus and passengers would pull in to await the arrival of the conductor – who would probably have hitched a lift on the next bus. It played havoc with CIE's scheduling, not to mention completely pissing off the passengers.

Mayhem and Fireworks

WITH THE FLURRY of another Christmas Eve upon us, our main priority was to ensure that, given the amount of booze lying around to supply the helpers, the father didn't have a relapse. The mother took each one aside separately and explained, but Boy-o-Boy had a major problem in coming to grips with the situation. He had only called a few times since the father had come back from 'drying out' and on his last visit had arrived so plastered that the mother ran him from the hall door before he even set foot in the house. But, as he had skin thicker than an old rhino, on Christmas Eve he bounced back in. Before the mother could send him on his way, he had infiltrated the crowd of helpers standing around in the kitchen awaiting the usual onslaught. Taking him aside, she began one of the strangest conversations I had heard up to that time.

'Look, Boy-o-Boy, the situation is that my husband can't be allowed any drink.'

'What? But it's Christmas, even Christ had a drink around this time.'

'Jesus Christ was just born, he would have been too young.'

'Yes, but as he got older, he must have celebrated his birthday with some fine whiskey.' And to reinforce this statement he dragged out a full bottle from one of his many pockets and waved it proudly in the mother's face. With anger now mounting in her voice she responded, 'Look, I don't care if Christ drank from Loch Erin, you are not to give Ron any drink, otherwise you can leave right this minute.'

'Boy, oh boy, Emily, why did He go to the bother of changing water into wine if He didn't want us to drink?'

Throwing up her hands in exasperation, she grabbed me and, standing me in front of him, instructed me to watch who he supplied with booze and to ensure that he didn't force any on the father. From what we could tell, it appeared that the father made it through that Christmas period without touching a drop; or if he did, he certainly kept it well concealed. That New Year's Eve – just as Gay Byrne was on the telly counting down the seconds to announce the impending hour . . . ten, nine, eight – the mother brought us all out onto the street, where, as if by some strange magic, the same telepathic message had been received by the rest of the residents. Front doors were opened up and down the street and people started to appear mysteriously, so that within seconds the emptiness was filled with jovial humanity calling out greetings to each other. The mother spotted Naty across the road and, as he had black hair, asked him to bring a lump of coal in from our backyard and place it on the mantelpiece. She said it would bring good luck to the house if a dark-haired stranger perform this old ritual and it should remain there until the next New Year's Eve.

January started very cold and icy, which was great as the buses couldn't run and I couldn't get to school. It suited me down to the ground, since my spelling hadn't improved one bit. Once again the teacher had turned his attention my way and had taken to ordering me to stand at the blackboard to spell words plucked from the air at random. There I would stand, at the head of the class in front of the blackboard, chalk in hands that were beginning to sweat so that the chalk stuck to them, while my face went bright red from embarrassment. Sensing the eyes of the rest of the class burning holes in my back and the suppressed hoots of laughter waiting to explode as soon as I had written the first letters in large capitals on the board.

'Heaps, spell "psychiatrist".' The first three letters I wrote would be sufficient to begin the afternoon's entertainment. As I painstakingly spelt out 'Sikietrest', I would hear the derision from everyone in the room and was consumed by feelings of embarrassment, turning to shame at having a brain that could understand and pronounce the word, but failed dismally to transmit this information into the correct written letters. Until eventually a feeling of anger would wash over me, causing me to snap the chalk against the blackboard and send it ricocheting over my head towards the first row of desks. Finally the priest, becoming bored with the entertainment, would send me back to my desk with a suitably scathing parting remark.

One evening I returned home from school and caught the tail-end of a conversation that my father was having in the shop with Inspector Malloy.

'. . . but we suspect that the hoodlums are from the flats behind us; they're becoming a complete menace to the area.'

'Agh, you don't have to tell me, Inspector. It's now deemed unsafe to use the toilets in the club on the weekends for fear of having a firework landing on your arse.'

'Well, don't worry, it's just a matter of time before we catch the delinquents and I will have great pleasure in reddening their arses before I bring them home to their parents, that's assuming the little bastards have any!'

After I had told Naty that the police were looking for us,

we both agreed to curtail our weekend entertainment, since it was only a matter of time before our luck ran out. But only a few days after making that resolution, as if they had a mind of their own, my feet dragged me once again into Moore Street 'just to see' what the banana-lady might have to offer as a substitute for bangers. Rockets were what she produced from a bag hidden under her stall, and as soon as I set eyes on them I stared in wonder at these objects that were capable of soaring to the heavens.

Three inches of red capsule attached to a long stick that, once set into an empty milk bottle, with a shower of sparks marking the course of the fuse, would blast itself free from its makeshift launch pad and rush into the night sky. Leaving a trail of yellow light behind to mark its arched course and then, finally, erupting with a shower of bright lights that would have extinguished and dwindled into darkness before the noise of the explosion reached our ears.

We had found our substitute for bangers and we let them off from the safety and seclusion of the old factory hidden behind the houses opposite St Michael's Church. I first came up with the notion, but it took Naty's courage to try it out, for as soon as I spoke the idea out loud the very thought chilled me. With Naty holding the milk bottle at arm's length, parallel to the ground, and me acting as loader and fuse-lighter, we discovered that we could launch a rocket horizontally. And after a few practice runs we could aim and fire the projectile accurately at any target we chose. In a flash of inspiration we realised that finally we had a missile we could launch into the interior of a bus with complete immunity from reprisal by a pissed-off conductor.

The following weekend, rearmed with a fresh bunch of Moore Street rockets (which smelled like overripe bananas), we installed ourselves behind the half-demolished wall that ran along the footpath from the dispensary nearly as far as the grounds of St Michael's Church. A year earlier all of the residents of Keogh Square had been moved out to Finglas and Ballymun, and the construction of the new flats had started. On completion they were to be given the highly original name of 'St Michael's Estate'.

We felt secure behind the wall, which was over 6 feet in height on the side against the footpath but only about 4 feet on our own side. And with plenty of space behind us to make a quick getaway into the construction site and lose any pursuer. Since there was a bus stop directly outside the church, we would have plenty of time to ready ourselves for our inaugural launch, and we settled down to await a bus with our arrangements carefully made.

Our plan was simple: wait for the bus to pass, thus offering us the best angle to fire our primed rocket in through the open platform at the rear. The rocket would hopefully whack into the conductor's area under the stairs, showering him with a bunch of sparks. Finally a bus showed itself but, as it had no passengers to collect or discharge, it roared past the stop without slowing down. So we didn't have a chance to ready ourselves and, cursing our luck, we once again settled down for another ten- to fifteen-minute wait. The footpath alongside the section of wall where we were hiding was in total darkness, since the streetlight close by was not working. Shortly after, a young couple out walking stopped suddenly when they drew level with our hiding place; the fellow grabbed his girlfriend and shoved her up against the wall. We couldn't hear anything for about a minute, except strange sucking noises (from our hiding place it sounded like a toy arrow with a wet rubber cap being removed from a pane of glass) until the girl broke the silence.

'Jesus, Jimmy, you're too rough.'

More sucking noises, the odd moan and rustle of clothes – and then a loud gasp from the girl made us both jump.

'No, Jimmy, me ma will kill me if she finds out.'

'You didn't say that the other night, me back is still bleeden' scratched.'

'Jesus, Jimmy, somebody will come along and catch us, ah Jesus, stop will you. Nooo Jimmy. Ah Jesus, hurry up, quick, before somebody comes along.'

More rustling noises, followed by grunting that reminded me of the sound the apes at Dublin Zoo made while being fed.

'Jimmy, you're hurting me, stop, Jesus, Jimmmmey. Oh Jimmy oh Jimmy, faster. Jesus faster, faster.'

It sounded to me like he was trying to knock her through the wall and, looking over at Naty who I could barely see in the shadows, it looked like he had gone into a trance. His tongue was hanging out of the side of his mouth and a huge bulge had appeared at the front of his trousers, which I thought strange. I hadn't a clue what the hell was happening at the far side of the wall, only that Jimmy was now making very strange noises that sounded like he was being choked to death. With a final drawn-out grunt from Jimmy, all movement and noise stopped and was replaced by heavy breathing.

'Jesus, Jimmy, you fecker, why did you stop?'

'I couldn't bleeden' help it. I didn't bleeden' well have one of them rubber things.'

'It'll be all right. The nuns told me that if you did it standing up and afterwards said three "Hail Marys", it'd be alright.'

'Jesus, is that bleeden' right?'

They started to walk off up the street. As they came under the one working streetlight we popped up our heads and, watching their retreating backs, caught a last statement from the girl.

'Ah Jesus, Jimmy, would you look, you fecker, you bleeden' well put a ladder in me nylons. Me ma will kill me.'

I asked Naty what the hell they had been doing. With his tongue still hanging out, he whispered in a hoarse voice, 'They were at it.' Before I could get him to expand on what 'at it' meant, a 21A bus pulled in at the church stop. As the bus passed by the closed paper shop, the bottle was already loaded with its missile and gripped in Naty's outstretched arms, with me holding the lighting match. Naty told me to light the fuse. The burning fuse glowed towards its destination as the bus passed our position with Naty tracking its rear entrance all the while, swivelling his body slowly just like the turret of a Second World War German Tiger tank. We could clearly see the conductor standing at his station under the stairs because the rear entrance was lit up like a Christmas tree. The fuse finally completed its journey and then, with a flash that turned our darkened area into an oasis of yellow light and temporarily blinded us, the rocket streaked outwards.

Just before the rocket ignited I noticed that Naty's hands were shaking like a weathervane in a force ten gale. Since we had previously practised this launch sequence, which he had then performed with rock-steady hands, I could only put his shakes down to what we had overheard a few minutes before. Later I should get him to explain what 'at it' meant, as I felt I was losing out somewhere there. In any case, he had missed the back of the bus by a mile; the rocket streaked off to the right of it and crossed the street, without appearing to slow down. It smacked into the side entrance of the Workman's Club, skidded off it and disappeared down the alley, out of sight, amidst a shower of sparks.

'Naty, what the fuck is wrong with you, you missed by a mile, are you blind or what?'

'It's ok, it's ok. I'll be alright next time.'

'You're shaking like a leaf and look at you, you're sweating like a pig, have you caught flu or what?'

'Shut up, just shut up and get ready, as there will be another bus along in a minute.'

'Do you want me to do it?'

'No, just shut the fuck up.'

Sure enough, within about ten minutes another bus arrived and, repeating our previous launch sequence, Naty succeeded in setting this one on its journey with steadier hands. It missed the conductor's head by inches, glanced off the bulkhead alongside his push-button bell, and rocketed into the downstairs interior of the bus. It worked its way up to the front, ricocheting off the roof and windows, before finally slamming into the partition that separated the driver from the passengers. With brake lights glowing and tyres squealing, the bus slewed across the road before screeching to a halt just opposite the Workman's Club. The driver jumped out, thinking that the shower of sparks he had seen in the coach behind him had been the bus on fire.

Coming around to the rear, he was met by a stunned conductor and a group of battle-axed, elderly female passengers, en route to their weekly bingo game. They were not a bit impressed and set about the still stunned conductor demanding, 'What the bleeden' hell did you let off? You could have killed the lot of us.' The driver, meanwhile, had gone up to the front of the bus and retrieved the remains of our missile; holding it up like a trophy, he handed it to the bingo group. Turning to the conductor he told him to get them all back on board, he was going to report this to the proper authorities.

'Bull's eye, bull's eye.' Our euphoria at having brought a Dublin bus to a halt quickly turned to dismay when the potentially dire consequences of the incident finally sank in: what if the rocket had ploughed into one of the women? We decided there and then to scrap any further assaults on buses. Since neither of us wanted to have anything more to do with the remaining rockets, we went down the laneway and slung them into the river, before heading off for our usual Saturday night treat, a bag of chips.

Knowing the father, he must have had a sneaky suspicion as to the identity of the gurriers throwing rockets around like confetti, for he insisted to the mother that I spend the Easter holidays in Tramore with the grandmother. The weather was appalling that fortnight, and this was probably the only reason I discovered the scam she was up to. To make matters worse, not only did my father know about it, but it was taking place with his explicit instruction.

It was pension collection day and the rain and wind pounded against the side of the caravan with such force that you wouldn't leave a dog out. So the grandmother sent me to the post office instead, to collect her money. She wrapped the pension books in a plastic bag along with a note for the postmaster, and gave me strict instructions not to open my mouth if asked any questions. On my way home curiosity took over and I decided to have a peek inside the bag. Instead of the two pension books I was expecting to see (I knew that she was also claiming a war entitlement from the British government), there were four. Apparently when old Claus had passed away the father had neglected to inform the Irish government of this fact; the death certificate had been issued from his own dispensary. Bemused by the grandmother's antics for the past number of years, I decided that my best course of action was to keep my mouth firmly clamped shut.

When I returned to school for the summer term I made a concerted effort to learn to spell properly. This I endeavoured to do by memorising the spelling of as many words as possible and completely ignoring the way in which we had been taught to break words down, syllable by syllable. By the end of the term I could remember the correct spelling of a lot of big words, but still completely messed up the smaller ones, often reversing some, or all, of the letters. But my renewed efforts appeared to satisfy my English teacher and, as I was quite proficient in most of the other subjects (except Irish), I came first in the class that year, beating off my archrival, Charley.

Apparently I had pipped first (in spite of my bad spelling) with the English essay I had written for the exam. My impressed teacher told the whole class that my essay was the product of 'a brilliant imagination showing a mind prepared to explore the improbable'. Then he made me read the story out to them all: it was the sad tale of an old woman living on her own in a caravan, battling against the elements, while ripping off two governments by claiming subsidies for a long-dead husband.

∞

One of my greatest wishes at that time was to be the proud owner of a push-bike. Any old push-bike, as long as it had two wheels, handlebars and a saddle. Earlier that year I had suggested to the mother that I might get a bike to ride to school. The idea was met with such a stern 'over my dead body' that even the father had reservations about ever bringing the subject up again. When he had mentioned it once before, the mother had asked him, 'Are you cracked or what? Him riding to school on a bike through the streets of Dublin? In God's name, are you trying to drive me mad?'

That summer passed quickly, with Naty and I experimenting in his basement at weekends with a new-fangled substance called sodium chlorate, which he had acquired from a chemist in town. Mixed with sugar, it burned fiercely like a fuse. We were also messing about with gunpowder, well, not exactly gunpowder, but its three main ingredients, for we were still trying to get the percentages right in the mix. All of our experiments to date had yielded nothing but a thick, black smoke cloud that had filled his house and driven his mother to bed.

I was now in fourth class with Mr Gleeson as our new teacher. As far as I was concerned, this moody, bad-tempered young tyrant brought a new reign of terror. He really did nothing out of the ordinary to instil such fear in me, but he certainly succeeded in petrifying me daily. With hindsight I can understand what triggered these feelings – my state of mind never really improved over the years, but luckily my reaction to a given situation did change. Back then I was a kid living in a perpetual state of dread, and that dread stemmed from the home front, where I continually expected an eruption of bad temper, either between my parents or directed at me. So, when everything was running smoothly, I worried about when it would revert to a situation of anger and accusation; and when the situation did revert to anger, I worried about what had been the cause.

And so every morning I sat in Mr Gleeson's class worrying (just like the rest of my classmates, no doubt) about the mood he would be in when he arrived. As I heard his footsteps advancing up the stairs, getting nearer and nearer, acid would begin to churn my stomach, travelling up into my gullet, souring my mouth and causing my breath to come in short gasps. If he arrived in a good mood, well, I just sat there all day petrified, wondering when he was going to throw a tantrum. Or if he arrived in a bad mood, dismay descended over the entire class – and doubled the acid being produced inside my own body. With my manifestation uncomfortably increasing in frequency over the first few months of the new term, I came up with a very simple solution. I wouldn't go to school. I would get off the bus in Harcourt Street and, instead of just walking past Stephen's Green, I went inside through the corner gate, hid my bag in a well-matured bush, and spent the morning walking along Grafton Street, visiting various shops.

I became a master at 'mitching' from school and quickly learnt the art of not getting caught. Any kid roaming the streets of Dublin with a school bag during school hours ran the risk of being approached by a garda and asked why he or she wasn't in school. But if you didn't have a bag on your person, well, the odds were in your favour that he would assume you were there with your parents' consent. Spotting priests and teachers from the school before they saw me was a more difficult task, and very quickly I learned to keep away from the main shopping streets near the Green, Dame Street or O'Connell Street. This tended to drive me into districts like North Wall and Ringsend, where some of the other kids I met 'on the mitch' definitely would not have passed my mother's questions with regard to their parents' origins or occupations.

I scraped by in this fashion for a time without getting caught and celebrated my tenth birthday with a gang of dockers down by the East Wall. The only handicap was the amount of time I had to spend in confession every Saturday, confessing the long list of lies I had told everybody that week; especially my mother, who would ask why didn't I have any homework for the night.

I finally returned to school in January, with the feeling that I was turning over a new leaf, and made a concerted effort to curtail my fear of the teacher. This was especially important as I was to make my confirmation that year, and the emphasis was on pounding a thicker version of the catechism into us. It didn't go too badly, because I had developed a retentive memory and could recite the lot from cover to cover without any problem. However, sometime during February, my old fears returned with a vengeance; and this time I quit going to school altogether – or at least that was my first intention.

I spent the first week freezing to death in the Phoenix Park; it was so cold I couldn't feel my hands. On my first day in the park I stayed in a public toilet that had large radiators supplied by 2-inch pipes running around the interior walls. I sat on the floor alongside one of the pipes, with my hands turning blue, and every few minutes I placed them on the pipes in the hope they would eventually heat up – which of course they never did. On one of my trips outside I was jumping up and down, trying to get the circulation back into my body, when I was spotted by a gardener. As soon as he saw me he blew his whistle and roared, 'Come back here, you little horror, you should be in bleeden' school.' I bolted with him giving chase, still blowing his whistle to attract other groundsmen, but I quickly lost him in a large grove of trees.

That weekend, on the Saturday, the father brought me up to the dispensary. Unlocking the door into the building, he astonished me by saying, 'Well Em, remember that day that we all went up the Dublin mountains and we came across the strange clearing in the middle of the forest, what did I tell you?'

'You told Catherine and me that it was a place where all of the fairies of Ireland meet.' Feeling proud that I had remembered.

'And what else did I tell you?'

Not having a clue as to where this was heading I continued, 'You told us a story of going somewhere similar with your father when you were a kid.'

'That's right,' he said. 'When I made my wish, I wished for a fob watch and within six months I received one as a present from an uncle that I didn't even know existed – and I bet that day you wished for a bike?'

Looking at my drooping jaw and smiling, he opened the

door into his office and, lo and behold, there stood a massive old black bike. Apparently, exactly one year earlier, he had found that particular bike in the yard of the dispensary, and when he had reported it to the police they had come to collect it. The father thought that would be the last he would ever see of it. But when nobody had reclaimed it from the Garda station after the required holding period of a year and a day, they had returned the bike to him, on the Friday, announcing that it was now his property. Overjoyed at the beautiful monster he was handing over to me, I broke down crying and told him about not having gone to school for the past week. When he asked me why, I could not find the right words to convey the reason, except just to say, 'I hate school.'

He sat me down and explained that we all have to do things we dislike and described how he hated going to work in the mornings and wished he didn't have to. So, telling me to 'act like a man', he said that he would give me a letter for the teacher explaining that I had been sick for the week. Returning to the matter of the bike, he said I could have it as long as I went to school, but we would have to hide it from the mother – and I wasn't to go and kill myself with it. Then he gave me a spare key for the dispensary, telling me to store the bike in the main waiting area; as the place was not open until ten in the mornings he thought no one would be the wiser. The following Monday I couldn't wait to get up and head off to school. With a nod of thanks to the father, I rushed out the door with his letter of excuse in my bag and took the beast out for our maiden voyage.

Cycling along the South Circular Road, I was completely oblivious to the cold that froze my hands to the handlebars, my eyes streaming in the icy wind, and my jacket flapping in the breeze. I felt a freedom and joy that I had seldom experienced before, which quickly turned to exhilaration. I soon learned how to duck and weave my way in, out and between the cars and buses of the traffic at the top of Harcourt Street, now beginning to slow down with the onset of the morning traffic jams.

For the next few weeks school became a temporary interruption to the feelings of anticipation that were with me constantly. During the night I looked forward to the morrow when I took to the roads again with the monstrosity. At school I awaited the bell announcing my freedom to once again learn new techniques for battling through the traffic. But the state of euphoria didn't last forever and slowly my consternation at having to face Gleeson every day returned and overrode the joy of cycling to his class. Until one day I realised that I could have the best of both worlds; I could simply ride the bike every day and just leave out the middle bit at school. Now I ventured further afield with the bike, and explored places that I had previously only heard about. Especially the posh areas where most of my classmates came from; now I was able to judge firsthand if those areas merited the amount of boasting that went with their addresses.

I kept this up for about two weeks with no clear view of how it was all going to end, only knowing that at least I felt a lot happier out and about on the bike. I didn't have to contend with the sickly acid feeling that I suffered constantly at school. But I also realised that, with every day I didn't go to school, I was getting deeper and deeper into a hole that I would not be able to climb out of. And then the inevitable happened.

One afternoon when I was pedalling down Rathmines Road I spotted Gleeson, who must have been taking an afternoon off himself. Certain that he hadn't seen me, I ducked down a side road, out of sight, but of course the sharp-eyed bugger had observed my exit. Gleeson put two and two together, what with me not being at school and then seeing me on the bike, and he wrote to the mother that same afternoon. When she received his correspondence she went straight over to the father's office and rang Gleeson on the school phone. Somewhere in the letter he had also mentioned the word 'bike'.

When I arrived home that evening, the parents, without saying anything else, told me to get into the car and we headed off towards town. With mounting fear, I realised our destination was CUS and slumped in the back seat. I recognised that this time there was to be no escape. I felt like a condemned man mounting the gallows as I was led into the now empty school, up the stairs, and into my classroom, where they had agreed to meet. Sitting with his arse hanging over one of the desks was Gleeson, smiling and nodding at the parents as if he was the best-humoured person in all the world. I felt relieved that finally it was all over, yet at the same time concerned at the possible repercussions. With the three of them now sitting on desktops, and me with my back to the blackboard, Gleeson proceeded to display a softness of character that I had never seen before.

After quietly pointing out to me that if I had continued without being apprehended, I would most certainly have missed out on my confirmation, he gently asked me why I had mitched from school. I was completely dumbfounded by his question and realised that if I blurted out that it was because of him, I would have nothing to back up my statement. I took the only course of action left to me: I shrugged my shoulders, said nothing, and continued to stare at the ground. When he and the mother had exhausted every conceivable reason they could think of, the father piped up with, 'Is it Mr Gleeson, Son?'

Hesitating for a second, with my mind screaming, 'Yes, it's because of that bad-tempered fucker', I looked directly at

Gleeson and shook my head. I could have sworn I glimpsed relief in his eyes. This seemed to alter the tempo of the meeting, because Gleeson jumped up and, rubbing his hands together, said, 'Well, all kids go through stages like this in their lives and since he hasn't missed that much schooling, we can certainly make sure he will be ready to make his confirmation. I'll give him extra homework, which he can do in the evenings to catch up on whatever he has missed.' And with that we were being shown the door. Feeling a lot better as I left than I had when I arrived, I suddenly remembered on our way back to the car that I wasn't out of the mess just yet. I still had the small matter of the 'non-existent' bike to contend with.

But I was, for the second time in as many hours, surprised by the mother's reaction and concluded that the father must have already tackled the subject with her. To my astonishment all she said was that I should reclaim the bike from wherever I had stored it so that she could look at it, and then she asked, 'Do you think me a complete fool altogether?' She had spotted the grease marks from the bicycle chain on my trousers and had known for months that I was riding a bike.

I can't say that anything changed in the classroom, nor did my fear lessen. The only thing I learned from the 'mitching episode' was to live with the fear – and that running away wasn't going to solve the problem. However, it was one thing preaching this, and an entirely different matter practising it. Still, I got up every day and, conquering my foreboding, I went to school.

∞

Eventually, the big day of our confirmation dawned. Over breakfast we were flabbergasted to hear on the morning news that the IRA had blown up Nelson's Pillar in O'Connell Street during the night. It had apparently scared the living daylights out of one of the few witnesses to the event, a taxi driver, whose interview was replayed over and over on every broadcast.

'Jaysus, I don't know how I wasn't killed. I had just driven by when the blast blew the fag outta me mouth, the noise of the explosion deafened me, and with the falling column following me up the street . . . shure, I thought I was gonna be crushed. And not a window on O'Connell Street broken. Can you believe that, wha'?'

When we arrived at school around ten o'clock, our pending confirmation forgotten with the excitement of events in the early hours of the morning, Gleeson formed us into our well-rehearsed positions. He checked us all like a sergeant-major getting his squad ready for inspection, verifying that we were correctly dressed and had our badges pinned to our lapels – badges that announced to the world that we were going to make our 'confo'.

With the news being passed from pupil to pupil that at two o'clock the Irish army were going to blow up the stump of what was left of old Nelson, we headed down Leeson Street to rendezvous with the girls from the Loreto Convent. They took up the rear, flanked by a company of nuns, and Gleeson took the lead with his head up in the air, swinging his umbrella to some rhythm that was pumping out in his own mind. En route to the cathedral our long column stopped traffic at every crossing.

When we arrived and entered the pews, Charley and I ended up on the outside, adjacent to the aisle. With the organ blasting out some hymn or another and flanked by a whole colony of priests, the bishop was led down the aisle to begin the ceremony. To our horror it was to include a High Mass, which meant that the bishop had better get a move on, as none of us wanted to miss the action at two o'clock on O'Connell Street. About halfway through the ceremony the bishop slowly made his way up the church, stopping at every pew and asking the first two occupants biblical questions. I nearly fainted with fright when he halted in front of us. He asked Charley some really daft question, like who made the world, then asked me mine. He glared at me because I had forgotten to join my two hands together in prayer, and in panic I rattled off an entirely incorrect answer to his question. This made his head jump back in total disbelief. For a second I thought his hat was going to fly off, but before he could say anything, with my face on fire from embarrassment, I babbled out the answer he wanted to hear and, patting me on the head, he moved on up the church.

I sat there thinking I could feel the eyes of the whole church on my back because I had stuffed up the answer, and so the rest of the ceremony passed in a haze. The only recollection I have is that when I left the church after the event I wondered why I didn't feel any different from when I had entered. We had been taught that, during the ritual, the tongues of knowledge from the Holy Spirit were supposed to descend from heaven and enter our heads, filling us with enlightenment.

Feeling a little bit cheated, I set off towards O'Connell Street, which had been blocked off with barricades on the southern end of O'Connell Bridge. I pushed myself through the mass of people who had gathered to watch the army do its job and ended up at the very front with an uninterrupted view of what was left of Nelson's Pillar. A little after two, with an army loudhailer starting a countdown, a sudden hush descended over the crowds: 'three, two, one . . .', and an immense cloud of white smoke enveloped the structure, followed seconds later by a sound like rolling thunder that washed over us and passed up the street. As the smoke cleared, revealing a pile of rubble scattered all over the road, people all around me exclaimed in excited voices:

'Jaysus look, they've busted all the windows in Clery's shop.'

'Bleeden' hell, you're right, and look, they smashed the GPO's as bleeden' well!'

'Jaysus, they should have gotten the IRA boyos back to finish the job, they blew the whole bleeden' thing up without cracking a pane!'

'Jaysus, you're bluddy right there.'

Leaving them to their chatter, I pushed my way out, walked into Dame Street and caught the bus home. There I was met by Catherine, who was waiting at the hall door for my return. Rushing to greet me, she threw her arms around my waist, announcing that we were to have our photograph taken together and that she would be four next week. Catherine's birthday was celebrated with a ceremony that the father had started with me at the same age: he stood her against the door dividing the kitchen from the shop, ensuring that her back was straight. He then marked her head height with the point of his pen and, moving her away, drew a line on the door with a ruler at the mark and wrote, 'Catherine, aged 4.' Catherine admired her height and pointed out that she was as tall as I was at the same age.

This led to a discussion as to how tall she would grow eventually, with the mother pointing out that her father was a tall man. The father said that, as all his family had always held on to their hair, the odds were that she would never go bald. This caused the mother to subconsciously finger Catherine's head as if to assure herself that she had a healthy head of the stuff.

A couple of weeks later I pedalled home for the holidays and flung my school bag under the dark recesses of the shop's counter, praying to the heavens that I wouldn't have to look at that bag again for at least another twelve weeks. To celebrate the occasion, I took Catherine up the street before the mother could stop us, and bought her an ice cream in the seated section of the Italian chipper on Tyrconnell Road. Watching her enjoying every mouthful, I reflected on the mother saying that she was not going to ruin Catherine as the father had ruined me at the same age.

I realised that my sister had the ability to enjoy every small treat that came her way with a pleasure that affected anyone lucky enough to be in her presence. I wondered what sort of brother I was going to be to Catherine; would she ever get married and would she have any children? Particularly since having kids seemed to involve the kind of shenanigans we had witnessed the night of the rocket on the bus.

The father had gone back on the booze, and the mother announced this to me not as if it were a condemnation, but as if it had been an agreement between the two of them. They had decided that he wasn't really an alcoholic after all, she confided. That he could, in fact, have a drink. And, since he was only drinking beer, well, there was no issue. And furthermore, the doctors hadn't known what they were talking about anyway. I reminded her of the AA meetings that we had attended together and how we had begged and begged him to quit. About the tears, and worry of him drinking us out of house and home, and all of the whiskey bottles that we had found hidden all over the house, and how the doctor had warned us that the father could never again touch the stuff. She kept repeating that he had been off it for a good while and, if he wanted, he could go off it again, but since he didn't have a problem, it wouldn't be necessary. That night the two of them went across the road to the upstairs lounge of the club, where they could keep an eye on the place and I could look after Catherine.

I found it incredible to think of the powers of persuasion that the man could use whenever there was a suggestion that he might be an alcoholic; if he had put his mind to it, he could have convinced the Pope that Christ didn't turn the water into wine at that wedding. And if there was ever a mention of what the doctors at St Pat's had said, he always responded that he had had to agree with them, otherwise they would not have let him out. Or some other story along those lines, depending on his frame of mind when the issue came up.

However, I have to admit that over the following summer he showed none of his previous symptoms of heavy drinking. A typical one was that he would answer in French when any of us asked him a simple question, such as 'What time is it?', or when someone told him 'dinner's ready'. And the more he was under the influence, the more mixed up his French became, until the time when I asked him if he wanted to watch telly and even I understood that his response translated as 'It is ten minutes past eight.'

So perhaps he had been right after all: all the doctors had been fools in their diagnosis and he could give it up any time he wanted. Perhaps I was just too sceptical. But I couldn't help thinking about the answer that the psychiatrist at St Pat's had given me when I had asked the question, what is the difference between an alcoholic and a boozer? With Boy-o-Boy springing to my mind, since he often gave it up for several weeks at a time. His answer to was, 'An alcoholic drinks to live, while a drinker lives to drink.'

I was still unsure into which category the father fitted.

Fire and Brimstone

TO THE PRESENT day the method of parking a car around St Stephen's Green has never changed: nose towards the kerb, with the arse parts sticking out. It works quite well, especially if all of the cars are roughly the same length. Coming out of Leeson Street one day, I pedalled like mad along the car-park side of the Green. I was hemmed in close to the car boots by traffic whipping past me on the outside and, glancing over at a car that was passing close to my leg, I failed to look ahead and notice that one parked car was sticking out further than the rest. I crashed right into its tail-lights, which stopped my bike dead in its tracks. I, however, continued, with my legs still driving imaginary pedals, until I came to a sudden halt as I met the asphalt on the far side, my right kneecap absorbing most of the impact.

Climbing to my feet, with the kneecap already blowing up like a balloon and turning an odd shade of purple, I picked up the bike (whose handlebars were rotated at a slight angle from the impact) and surveyed the damage to the car. Well, for one thing, the car's owner was certainly going to be annoyed when he returned, for all that remained of his right-hand rear-light section was lying on the ground in a shower of red, yellow, and white pieces of smashed glass that winked back at me. And whereas the owner might previously have boasted about the fine lines of his car's bodywork, that was now interrupted by a very deep dent, compliments to the handlebars.

Expecting to be apprehended at any moment by someone looking for the culprit, I grabbed my school bag (now lying in the middle of the road where passing cars were dodging it), collected the bike, and attempted to beat a hasty retreat from the immediate area. But, as I mounted the machine again, I nearly fell off for the second time. It was clear that my right leg was not responding to the instructions being transmitted from the brain.

I straightened the handlebars by jamming the front wheel into the railings of St Michael's Church and tugging on them until they were re-aligned, and then pedalled off home where I managed to hide my injury from the mother for the whole evening. But when I woke up the following morning my right knee had seized up to such an extent that I could not stand up unless I hopped on one foot. Catherine raced off to call the mother who, with the aid of her nursing skills, decided that while it was not busted the damage was sufficient to keep me from school for at least a week. After they had taken me to the dispensary for Dr Dillon to confirm the mother's diagnosis and strap up my knee, the parents decided that we should make the most of my incapacity and the Indian summer we were experiencing, so we all headed down to visit the grandmother in Tramore for the remainder of the week.

The weather was fantastic for the whole week, with not a breath of wind blowing, allowing us to sunbathe in the sanctuary of our little cul-de-sac without worry of being interrupted by any passers-by. My knee had healed perfectly and we spent our days either swimming in the sea, or lounging around outside the caravan. We were parked at the end of the cul-de-sac, on the left-hand side, leaving a 4-foot gap in front of the door that faced the ditch. There was also a space of roughly 20 to 30 feet between the front of the caravan and the berm that blocked us off from the main road, with about the same distance from the right-hand side of the caravan to the opposite ditch. At the end of the hitch on the caravan rested a yellow Calor gas bottle connected to the van with a long rubber hose.

The morning of the 20 September 1966 promised that the day would be as hot as the last days had been; there had not been a breath of air throughout the night and, as the day advanced, it became hotter still. An eerie silence descended on the place, as if the birds themselves were too drowsy to announce their presence. The grandmother was sitting indoors, and the father had removed one of the foam seats that doubled as a bed and placed it on the ground for Catherine to lie on, directly between the gas bottle and the berm. As soon as I spotted Catherine getting what I considered to be a prime lounging area, I felt jealous and asked the mother if the two of us could go and play. She was sitting by the right-hand side of the caravan in a deck chair and refused my request. I was the one, she commented, who had crashed off the bike (which she had never wanted me to have in the first place) and bashed my knee (still supposed to be injured), so I could just sit down and behave myself. Grabbing an empty milk crate, I retrieved an old comic from the back of the car and stomped over to the far side of the clearing, directly opposite Catherine. I watched the father retrieve his Primus stove from the boot of the old Popular and set about boiling a kettle to make a pot of tea. This stove was his pride and joy and was about a foot square, with a fold-up lid that acted as a windbreak when opened and a little holding tank for the pint of methylated spirits on which it ran. It had only a single burner ring and there was barely enough room on that for an average-sized kettle. Once it was lit, it produced a small blue flame that would eventually bring the kettle to the boil, as long as you were very patient and not gasping for a cup.

I watched him, over the top of my comic, as he went through the ritual of preparing the little stove for its task, which involved priming the thing by pumping up and down on a little piston that was fitted to the side. He glanced at Catherine, who appeared to be asleep on her makeshift sunbathing bed, then stood up, retrieved a box of matches from his pocket, bent down, and struck a match.

A ball of bright yellow flame whooshed directly towards me right across the clearing, with a sound like an approaching express train, and physically plucked me off the crate I was sitting on, blasting me against the ditch. Temporarily blinded and deafened by the blast, I picked myself off the ground, trying to see through eyes that could barely make out a grey, out-of-focus landscape. The clearing was still, as if time had stopped and I was the only person capable of movement.

The first of my senses to recover were those of smell and taste, and my mouth seemed to be filled with the flavour of burned smoke. Then a sickly sweet smell of burning flesh and hair filled my nostrils, as if somebody somewhere was overcooking the fat of a pig they had left on the fire for too long.

Looking down, I saw the skin on my chest was spitting and bubbling with the flames shifting up and down my torso; sensing a tickling sensation around my ankles, I also noticed that I was standing in a sea of yellow flames that were dancing across the ground. Finally I realised that I was on fire and remembered the small stream that wound its way through the woods a couple of hundred yards down the road. My body was screaming at my brain to put the fire out as I dashed through the gap in the berm – and ran, and ran, and ran, not even realising that I was running with bare feet on the gravel that made up the hard shoulder of the road.

Reaching the small stream, I ran into the water, unable to register its icy chill, only that it was wet. Then I threw myself down, ignoring the sharp stones on the river bed, and rolled over and over until I put out the flames, causing steam to rise from my skin. My body now seemed to be without feeling and, still not comprehending exactly what had happened, I decided to return to the caravan in the hope that someone there could explain the last five minutes.

I ran back up the road and arrived just in time to see the father helping the mother into the back seat; she was cradling a bundle shrouded in a blanket. He spotted me just as he was getting into the driver's seat and shouted that if I wanted to go with them, I should hurry up and get into the car straight away. I couldn't hear him properly because my ears were still ringing with a high-pitched buzzing noise and I was barely able to see his wild-looking face with my still half-blinded eyes. But I made out that he was frantically gesturing at me and pointing to the passenger door, so I ran towards it.

I climbed into the back seat and, for the first time, realised that it was Catherine who was wrapped in the blanket that the mother was cradling. She was very quiet and, looking directly at me with her large, grey eyes, she smiled at me as if she had seen something amusing. Looking down at myself, I noticed for the first time that what I could see of my body was, for some reason, completely black, as if I had spent the day working in a coal mine. And the pair of shorts I had been wearing were so badly tattered that I was amazed the mother hadn't given out to me about ruining them – and why were we driving with all of the windows open?

The mother was talking over father's shoulder from the back seat and, as some degree of my hearing began to return, I could hear her say that she was not too happy about

Catherine and could he drive faster. The father was bare-chested, I noticed. With that, I passed out, dreaming that we were all just going for a drive. I came to with a shuddering of the wheels, as if we had bumped across some sort of high kerb. For a few seconds I thought that the dream was reality, and that whatever had happened to me was the dream, until I was once again over-powered by the stinking smell of burning hair and flesh. I wondered why my lips hurt, why was I so cold, and why did my face feel so stiff?

The father pulled into a petrol station on the outskirts of Waterford to ask directions to Ardkeen Hospital, roaring his question through the passenger window at some people who were standing at the petrol pumps. They responded with hand signals and, without acknowledging their assistance, he bounced and bumped his way back onto the road. Within minutes we roared through the gates of the hospital and pulled up in front of the casualty department. There, before the car had even come to a stop, a nurse, doctor and two orderlies ran out to us. The father shrugged off their offers of assistance and reached into the back seat, gently lifting Catherine out and holding her to his chest, then running in through the doors with the hospital staff chasing after him, followed closely by the mother.

Climbing out, I thought that I should also head in after them, since I was beginning to be aware of a pain, the like of which I had never experienced before. Just inside the double doors of the entrance a wide corridor ran off into the distance, and to the right of this was a room with a large glass window, through which I could see that Catherine had been laid on a surgical table. They had removed the blanket from around her and, to my amazement, I noticed that she was completely naked.

As I walked into the room, I was torn between wondering

what I was doing there and if I should flee before I was spotted, and bewilderment as to where Catherine's clothes had gone. But even in the short distance from the car to the room feelings had begun to return to my body, sending messages to the brain that somehow I had been injured – and then the pain hit me.

It attacked everywhere at once; I felt as if my whole body was cooking slowly over an open coal fire. Still nobody had noticed me and so I climbed up onto the long row of cupboards that ran under the window. Putting my left hand to my head, I realised that I had no hair and, touching my scalp, bawled out with the pain. That made everyone at the table jump and turn in my direction.

First the mother begged someone to give me something for the pain – and then she told me to shut up and be quiet, couldn't I see that my sister was seriously injured? I tried to curtail my sobbing and shook with cold and fear, since I had not yet come to terms with what had transpired. What did it matter what had happened to Catherine? Could they not see how much I was hurting? The room became darker and the voices faded away in the distance as, lying down on the counter top, I drifted off into merciful darkness.

I found myself in a deep well that was completely black and, miles above my head, there was a very bright light surrounded by a dark rim, as if the sun was shining high in the sky. It bathed the area above me with light that only penetrated a little way down into the void where I was. All of a sudden a head appeared over the rim and smiled down at me. Realising that it was Catherine, I wondered what she was doing up there and, more importantly, why was I in this hole with no hope of getting out?

The well was very cold and there was a smell of rotting eggs. I was still freezing cold when I became aware that I was in a bed – that much I could tell from the feeling of starched linen against my back – but I had no idea if it was day or night, since my eyes were covered with heavy bandages. The smell was over-powering. It was not now of rotting eggs, but of burnt hair, and it seemed to be coming from my own forehead, which felt tight and wrinkled. There was movement in the room and I heard my father's voice. I felt hands carefully turn me over on my side, then the sharp jab of a needle being stuck into my backside.

I was back in my well again, looking up at the bright light that never changed in intensity. But now it was hurting my eyes and I was engulfed by an overwhelming fear because I was convinced I was going to die. I knew that I didn't want to die because I was frightened of dying. But I was slipping further down into my hole in the ground, and I kept on losing the bright light within the rim high above, which caused me to panic. I had the feeling that if I lost that light I was doomed to spend the rest of my existence in this black void. But the light remained. I couldn't get rid of it and it began to give me a constant headache. No matter how tightly I tried shutting my eyes, the light still burned through as if burning a hole in the back of my head. And the smell was always in the background, sometimes exploding to the fore and over-powering me with its stench.

The bed was rolling; I could feel movement and my first thought was that at least I was being transferred away from the bright light and the awful stench of burning hair. But the light and the smell followed me along a corridor that seemed to go on forever. Doors banged against the side of the bed when we passed through, as if the bed itself had been used as a battering-ram. Voices instructed my bed-pushers to gently lift me up and place me on an ice-cold slab in a room that felt beautifully cool. A woman's voice told me to be very still because they were going to X-ray me – and not to worry, as I was going to be alright.

When I tried to ask the voice (before it faded away into the gloom) if it could put out the bright light and eliminate the smell, I found that I could think the words but not form them with my mouth; instead all that came out was a choking noise. Turning my face to see if that would help my speech, I felt gentle but firm hands placed on the wad of bandages around my head and that same voice said, 'Now, just be quite still, and we will have you out of X-ray soon.'

All at once I awoke with as much shock as if I had been catapulted out of my well like the shell of a large-calibre gun and dumped on the ground in the sunlight. What's more, it seemed that the friction of this sudden discharge had scorched my body and melted the flesh on the front of my torso. And then I felt the bandages being removed gently from my eyes; my first sight was the face of a nun looking down at me.

Jesus Christ, what the hell is Sister Charlotte doing here and how did I get back to Goldenbridge School? I thought I had moved on from there? Very slowly the nun came into focus and I realised, with relief, that it wasn't Sister Charlotte after all, only somebody that looked like her.

'Merciful God, Doctor, but I think he will be able to see again, at least from the right eye.'

'DV, sister, DV. Now remove the bandages from the left eye.' These words came from a voice a little way off and behind her. With the bandages removed, the eye surgeon came into view. (I only remember hearing him called DV, which I later found out is the Latin abbreviation for 'God willing'.) Leaning over my head, he peered into both eyes and, grunting with satisfaction, he complemented the nun on her good work, then left the room without another word.

'I'm going to leave the bandages off now, as your eyes need

oxygen and, merciful God in heaven, but it's nothing short of a miracle, an absolute miracle . . . but I knew the holy water would work. I will be back tonight to bless them again.'

Making the sign of the cross over me, she went over to the other bed in the room, which I realised held my father. After checking the dressing on his chest, she whispered something to him, before leaving with a whoosh of her long, black dress. I was in a small room with white walls, ceiling and floor; my bed was pushed right up against the left-hand wall, leaving the door to the room directly at the end of my bed. Across to my right was a larger bed containing the father who was gazing at me and grinning, as if he was glad to see me. As soon as our eyes met he said, 'Welcome back to the land of the living, Son. How are you feeling? You had us worried there for a bit.'

Well, that was a good question, how was I feeling? I didn't know, so I started to explore the situation. I was in a cage; well, not exactly in a cage, rather one had been placed over me with a single, white blanket on top, so that it was as if I was lying naked inside a small tent that was draughty and cold. From what I could see of my body through my right eye, all of my top half was covered with squares of sticky, orange gauze that had been placed over me like a patchwork quilt.

Since I couldn't see or feel my legs or feet, I couldn't check their condition. As I became more and more aware of my surroundings, I began to feel a strange sensation over the top half of me, including the top of my head, which began as a sort of low, pulsating pain that accelerated quickly, causing me to cry out. Until it finally settled down to a constant throbbing, at which point I heard the rattling of a trolley as the door opened and a nurse approached with a syringe. Thankfully, before she reached the bed I drifted into darkness, only this time I must have slept, because I never again saw my well.

The following days in hospital settled into a routine that I marked off into three sections during my waking hours – 8 a.m., noon, and 6 p.m. – since these were the times for my injections, and I came to hate them more than my captivity. I woke up in the morning to a nurse turning me over on my side and jabbing me with a needle. Then spent the rest of the day, in dread, listening for the noise of the trolley marking her return for the next injection. My arse became so bruised that in the end the nurses had difficulty finding an unused spot. After the stabbing, the blanket and cage would be lifted off and the sticky, gauze patches would be removed with tweezers, my skin sprayed with an ice-cold substance, and new patches applied. At eight o'clock every evening the nun reappeared and anointed my eyes with holy water.

My feet aroused the most interest, especially in the doctor and his apprentices who crowded around the end of my bed each morning during the doctor's rounds. Since I couldn't see or feel anything in that area, this didn't bother me at all. I was heavily sedated and so the significance of the situation was lost on me. As it turned out, they were worried about whether or not I would walk again.

The doctors never seemed to do anything for themselves: once they were all jammed into the tight space around the end of my bed, a nurse would have to fight her way through the mob to lift up the sheet, which she would drape over my tent. Then the head doctor would address the mob, explaining that before them was a young boy who was a burn victim. And, to ensure that all of them grasped the situation, he would continue, '. . . and, as you can see, while having sustained third-degree burns to his upper body, his ankles and feet have sustained burns to the . . .'; here he always lost me, since it all sounded like Greek. Picking each of my feet up by the big toe, he'd haul them into the air, as if raising the tail of a horse to

show its rear end to some prospective buyer. With that, the
rest of them would push and shove each other out of the way
in their eagerness to peer at the prize on display. Without so
much as a 'good morning to you', he would then drop my feet
and march out of the room with the rest of them scurrying
after him.

The father had also been slightly injured in what was now
officially referred to as the 'explosion', taking the lead from
newspaper and TV coverage of that fateful day. I had been
placed in the father's room so that he could keep an eye on my
condition; likewise the mother was installed in Catherine's
room, to perform a similar task, although she herself had been
uninjured in the explosion. As I began to be given the details
of the story, I discovered that Catherine was in much more
serious shape than I, owing to her age, but her condition was
now being described as 'stable'.

At times during the day our room was crowded with
people from the Gardaí, who were carrying out a full
investigation, or insurance agents and representatives from the
Calor Gas company, all of whom were trying to fit the pieces
together to discover the cause of the explosion. When asked
for my opinion, I could only choke out 'a blinding ball of
flame hit me', by way of explanation for the whole saga.

At first they tried to pin the blame for the catastrophe
firmly on the shoulders of the father. At one point they (being
Calor Gas) suggested that, since he had been lighting the
Primus stove at the time, it was in fact this object, filled with
its pint of methylated spirits, that had caused the fireball and
not their Calor gas bottle, as previously suggested in the news.
At which the father threw his bedpan at them. It missed and
bounced off the back wall, but it was enough to send the two
agents running out of the room and that was the last we saw
of them. The father's reaction was based on Garda findings in

the course of a thorough inspection of the scene of the explosion.

They had found a small hole, the size of a pinhead, in the top of the gas bottle, which apparently had been the result of corrosion. The father had only replaced the gas bottle a few days before, and it had been leaking slowly over the couple of days leading up to the 'big bang'. With the weather being so nice, and especially as there had been not a breath of wind, the gas had settled on the ground, spreading unnoticed as the bottle discharged its deadly substance. Gas companies only gave their products an odour after our accident, and so our bottle continued to leak undetected.

Catherine, who had been lying on a foam mattress a few inches off the ground, was, in effect, lying in the gas layer. As soon as the father struck the match, she was engulfed in a mass of flames that consumed the mattress in seconds, nearly incinerating her, and resulting in burns to over 70 per cent of her body. The father, who had been stooping over the cylinder while attempting to light the small stove, had received burns to his chest and right arm as a result of the initial ignition of gas that was still escaping from the hole in the top of the bottle. Once ignited, it had flared back at him in its attempt to suck oxygen from its immediate surroundings, before exploding out in a fireball across the clearing towards me.

If I had been sitting a few feet to either side, the jet of burning gas would have missed me completely and exhausted itself against the far ditch. This was corroborated by the position of the burns to my body, since they showed the fireball had hit me full in the chest, face and head, leaving my left arm unscathed, while badly burning my right. The damage to my feet and ankles resulted from standing in the layer of burning gas near the ground.

The grandmother, who had been inside the caravan at the

time, was, of course, unscathed. Similarly the mother, who had been sitting on a deck-chair at the side of the caravan with her feet elevated, had received no injury. But to a certain extent she had suffered the greatest shock, as she had heard the loud bang and been temporarily blinded by the ball of yellow flame that shot across her vision, obscuring the clearing. Regaining her senses quickly, with all of the bushes surrounding the clearing on fire, the mother had rushed into the smoke and spotted Catherine lying on the smouldering remains of the mattress, with her dress completely burned from her body.

When she searched and could not find me, she assumed that I had disobeyed her instructions and gone off playing, thus escaping the whole event. Realising immediately that Catherine was seriously injured, her nursing training kicked in: she knew that she would have to stabilise Catherine's condition before she could attempt to move her, as she had gone into shock. Thus there was a time lag, during which I galloped off down to the stream to quench myself and then returned. Otherwise, unknowingly, they might have driven away without me.

When the father spotted me returning, he assumed that I had been playing because I was black from head to toe. His invitation to get into the car had been snapped at me for that reason. It was only when I had walked myself into the casualty department that any of them realised that I, too, had been involved. A kind of a comedy of errors.

Ten days after we had been installed in Ardkeen Hospital, it was announced that both my sister and I were stable enough to be transferred to hospitals in Dublin. Somehow or other I got hold of a comic; I had been warned repeatedly not to hold one, because if the ink got on my hands they might become infected. I remember one of the ambulance drivers handed it to me after they had loaded me into the back of the ambulance on a stretcher. Then, securing me on the left-hand side, they went off to fetch Catherine. It was a magnificent day and the sun was shining beyond the double doors of the ambulance, which had been left open. We were backed up immediately in front of the hospital's main entrance and, peering out, I felt that it was too nice a day to be taking a trip to Dublin, especially as we didn't know which hospital we were being taken to. Finally they wheeled Catherine out and placed her on the opposite bunk, strapped her in and closed the doors, and I felt the van shake as they climbed into the front. Away we went, with sirens howling.

Looking across at her, I thought they had brought the wrong person, as the girl I was looking at seemed to have grown; this wasn't my sister at all. With panic setting in, I was just about to start shouting at them through the partition to stop, when she turned her head towards me and said, 'Nn, Nn', and, ever so slowly, I realised that this person on the other bed really was her. She appeared to have changed much in those past ten or twelve days. I had no idea how long we had been in the hospital; if a stranger had asked me I would have guessed at least a few months. But looking closely at her through my left eye (which still was not working too well), I saw that her face had become thinner and she looked much older, as if during the stay in hospital she had matured from a child into a young girl. There wasn't a mark on her face and her hair also seemed longer. I felt comfortable about her condition, because, from what I could see, there didn't appear to be a lot wrong with her.

I wondered where the parents had got to and why nobody was travelling in the ambulance with us? There was a space of about two feet between Catherine and I, and every time I looked in her direction she choked out words in a strange voice that definitely didn't sound like her at all. She wanted

me to hand her over the comic to look at it. Playing the role
of big brother, I told her 'no' repeatedly, explaining that the
ink would get on her hands and we would both get into
trouble – I wasn't even supposed to have it in the first place.
Then, once more engrossed in the antics of 'Desperate Dan',
I didn't notice Catherine's hand slide out from under her
blanket and reach across the gap that separated us.

It was a claw that grabbed the top of the comic: her right
hand was hooked in a fixed, rigid position and none of her
fingers were working. The skin on her hand and (as far as I
could tell) her arm was a pinkish colour, as if it was new.
Staring at the disfigurement, I recoiled from her in case the
skin touched me. The hand was pulled back and I jammed the
comic down between my bunk and the wall, as if placing it out
of sight would make her forget it. Lying there staring across at
her, I experienced an overwhelming feeling of shame, for I had
drawn back in horror from my own sister. I wondered if I
should bring the comic back out and hand it over to her. But
I realised that she would probably not be able to hold it.

I began to cry. I had no idea why I should be so upset, as
all I really wanted to do was reach across and hold her, but as
soon as I felt that urge I remembered the claw-like hand and
knew that I would recoil from it again. So I cried for her, I
cried for her not having a brother to be there for her when she
most needed it, I cried because I was ashamed of myself. I cried
because I was nothing but a small, selfish boy who was only
concerned about his own injuries. I cried because I didn't
know where my parents were and why they weren't in the
ambulance with us. I cried because Catherine was smiling
across at me and there was I acting like a big baby – and when
that thought hit me, I was finally able to stop crying.

The ambulance went directly to St Stephen's Hospital,
down by Kingsbridge railway station, and as soon as we pulled

in the door was opened by two nurses and a doctor who climbed into the back and went over to Catherine. After examining her for a few minutes, the doctor called in the ambulance men and instructed them to remove the stretcher. The last I saw of my sister was her stretcher being rushed through the hospital doors and disappearing from sight, with the two nurses running after their new charge. Expecting them to come back for me, I was amazed when the doors of the ambulance were closed again and, with the sound of the passenger and driver doors slamming, we were on the move once more. All alone in the back of the van a feeling of loneliness and abandonment washed over me; I had no idea even where they were taking me.

Shortly after, when I peered out of my window, I recognised the entrance to St James's Hospital. We stopped by Hospital 7 casualty unit, where my two drivers unloaded me and wheeled me along a corridor to a room with six curtained cubicles. Picking one as if by random, they placed me on the bed, wished me luck, and departed.

As time ticked slowly by, I began to think that perhaps nobody knew I was there. Since I couldn't walk, I had visions of nobody finding me for a few days; then, when they did find me, perhaps they wouldn't know what to do with me? After what seemed an eternity, the curtain was flung back and a nurse poked her head in saying, 'Ah, there you are, we were wondering what had happened to you.' Closing the curtain again, she disappeared for a few more minutes before returning with a doctor in tow. He read the file that the drivers had left at the bottom of my bed, then examined me and, after tut-tutting at the state of my dressings, told me that there would be no more bandages. They were now going to allow nature take its course. Finally, issuing instructions to the nurse, he left with a rustle of his white coat. Alone with the nurse, my first thought was to ask if I would be given any more injections. When she said no, I felt relief for the first time since the accident because at least that particular horror was over.

I was moved upstairs to a ward containing six beds and installed in a corner bed near the corridor. I didn't really take note of the other occupants of the room until later on that evening, when I discovered that I had been shoved into a geriatric ward. In spite of my injuries and the fact that I couldn't walk, I was probably the fittest person there. For the few nights I spent in that ward, I didn't get a wink of sleep from the racket the others made.

First of all, the lights were left on throughout the night and, when I used the call button over the bed to request that the nurse put the lights out (the only time I used it during my entire stay in hospital), I was informed that it was 'hospital regulations' to leave them on, as the nurses and patients needed to see where they were going throughout the night. But she agreed to place a towel over the light nearest to my bed, which promptly fell off as soon as she left.

The noise began from the bed to my immediate left and continued around the room, echoing off the walls, and sounding as if the inmates were rehearsing for a job in the sound effects department of a film studio. 'Phhhooooooooooooo . . .' I thought that the old fellow next to me had ripped his bed sheets in half until the smell hit me. Then I realised what he had done, which was quickly repeated by the other four, until it sounded like the wind instrument section warming up in an orchestra.

'Phhhooooooooooooo . . ., brrraaaaaaaaaa . . ., faaaaaaaaaaaaaaaaa . . ., phuuuuuuuuu . . .' This lasted for at least five minutes, varying in tempo and length, until they wore themselves out with the effort and the room smelt like an old tannery factory. Thinking that they had blown themselves to sleep (and slowly recovering from the smell), I resigned myself to sleeping with the light on. The next act lasted for the rest of the night with the odd intermission. Each of them fell out of bed at some stage or another and stumbled their way to the toilets (which were somewhere out in the corridor), managing to knock against every other bed in the room, both while leaving and returning.

'Haaaahaaaahaaaa . . ., Haaaahaaaahaaaa . . .' (as the bed-head banged against the wall), 'Haaaahaaaahaaaa, Haaaa-haaaahaaaa . . .' Until, finally, one of them succeeded in dragging up the phlegm that must have been lodged somewhere around his feet and spat it out into a bedpan, making as much noise as if a bullet had been fired into it. As soon as dawn broke it was if a switch had been hit and all noise ceased completely. Thinking that at last I could get some sleep, I had just settled down when I was aroused by the sound of a trolley being bounced into the ward by a lovely old woman. She had a cigarette hanging out the side of her mouth and sounded like she should be selling bananas and bangers on Moore Street.

'Mornin', mornin', and who have we here? Jaysus young fella, you look awful, what in the name of Jasyus happened ya? Do you want some tay? Aagh, God love ya. Jaysus, did you get hit by a bleeden' bus, or wha'? Ha, ha.'

Before I could answer, one of the old-timers piped up, 'Quiet Molly, can't you see he's trying to sleep. The poor boy has been out to the world since they brought him in yesterday. Shush now and leave him rest.'

'Don't you tell me to shush, you bleeden' old fart or you'll get no breakfast. Tom, did you sleep well? I hope you weren't dreaming of me like youse always do? Haw, haw.'

This was followed by a hacking cough as if she smoked about eighty Woodbines a day.

Molly abandoned her breakfast trolley in the middle of the ward and started to distribute trays to the patients, exchanging jokes and banter with the other geriatrics on a level that suggested they had been in the ward for a long time. Finally, approaching my bed, she put down a tray with a cup, saucer, a side plate with two slices of bread, and a larger plate containing . . .; well, I have no idea, as it looked a bit like scrambled egg, except that it was in one large lump and was the wrong colour. There were also two black objects (which I hoped were what passed for sausages) and something else that looked like it belonged on the bottom of somebody's shoe. I told her that I wasn't hungry, so she sat down on my bed and, taking another fag from behind her ear, said, 'Now look here, sonny. If youse don't bleeden' ate up, youse can't expect to get bleeden' better, now can ya?'

I have to admit that it didn't taste as bad as it looked and, while I was ploughing through the 'breakfast', Molly returned with the biggest teapot that I had ever seen: so large, in fact, that she had to hold it up with both hands. She filled my cup to the brim, which caused half of the contents to spill over into the saucer, and, with a final wave at everybody, she rattled and banged her way out of our ward. On into the next one, where I could hear her begin her morning banter all over again.

The medical staff reintroduced my thrice-daily injections the next morning because I had caught another infection. I blamed Molly's breakfast. And so the horror of having to pass the days waiting for the sound of the trolley that announced the administration of those wretched jabs began all over again. I don't remember seeing the parents during the few days that I spent with the geriatrics; I guess they were too tied up with Catherine. Thankfully, on the morning of day four, two orderlies appeared in my room and announced that they were taking me to another ward.

Molly turned out to be every ward's equivalent of the town crier, as she knew everything about every patient and, of course, more than the doctors. 'Shure, Jaysus John, I could have told ya that ya had bleeden' gallstones from the look of youse when they first brought you in. Didn't me Auntie May, God love her, die of 'em only last year and the fecking doctors couldn't save her. Aagh Jaysus, but they never listen to me. Take me word for it, if they bleeden' well operate on ya, youse'll be fecked.'

So much for her bedside manner; she had everybody terrorised with stories of her family's illnesses. From the talk out of her every one of her relations and friends must have had one or more of every symptom under the roof of the hospital and, worse still, most had died from them. Before the first day was out, Molly had the complete history of what had happened to me and where my sister was.

'Shure, no wonder yer parents haven't come to visit ya, God love 'em; they must be sitting day and night with yer poor little sister. What age was she again? I'll say a prayer for her on me way home tonight at the chapel.'

Molly's visits became one of the highlights of the day, as, apart from listening to her chatter, there was not a lot to do but lie down and read from one of the books I had taken from the hospital's mobile library that rolled around the wards every afternoon. This service was run by a Molly look-a-like called Mary, who I swear couldn't read, because she kept handing me books written in Irish. The second afternoon after I was settled in my new ward, either Molly was early, or Mary was late. In any case, the pair of them arrived in the ward together and decided to wreak havoc on one of the patients.

'Jaysus, howaya Mary? Give us a bleeden' light and keep away from tha' fella over there, or he'll try and pinch yer arse.'

'Pinch me arse? Jaysus, I'll give him a good clout across the bleeden' ears. Here, give us a fag will ya? Aagh, fuck it, I'm bleeden' well burned out from 'em.'

'Jaysus, Mary, did ya hear how the fecker broke his bleeden' leg?'

'Jaysus no, Molly, tell us. Did he fall off his missus while riding her? Ha, ha, ha.' Her laughter developed into a barking cough, with Molly snorting like a pig digging up the ground with its snout. All the while the 'fella', whose name was Mike, was quietly reading his paper and completely ignoring the two women who had taken up residence in the middle of the floor with the full attention of the rest of the ward.

'Well Jaysus, Mary, yer nearly rite there. He was in bed when he busted it, issen that right Mike?'

'How can ya break yer bleeden' leg while in bed, Molly? Hey Mike, tell us how ya could break yer bleeden' leg in bed; is she having me on or wha'?'

Mike continued to ignore them and took an even greater interest in the paper he was reading. Molly continued with the fag stuck out of the side of her mouth as her left hand adjusted the rollers in her hair underneath a scarf knotted below the chin. From the rear she looked like she was rooting under a brooding hen in search of eggs.

'He turned over in bed and broke it.'

'Agh, feck off, yer havin' me on. Hey young fellow, have ya finished reading that book I gave ya?'

'Look, I'm telling ya, there was a hole in the bleeden' sheet which his big toe got stuck in, and during the night he turned over and woke up the next morning with his leg busted.'

'Jaysus, is tha' rite? Hey, Mike, is tha' rite? Jaysus, wha' sort of eejit are youse anyway? Yer better take them sheets home with ya, or next time ya might get your bleeden' head stuck in it? Ha, ha, Molly, wha'? Ha, ha, ha. Hureeee hureeeee . . .' (as another fit of coughing racked her).

The doctors here were no better than in the last place when it came to their morning visits, only this time the fellow I saw appeared to have a deal more apprentices following him around. He also had the ward sister in attendance. Once again my feet became their centre of attention: they now took to jabbing them with pins and tapping them repeatedly with small hammers, checking for some reaction from me. They had stopped applying the yellow sticky stuff to my chest, so the burns were drying up and had been replaced by thick, black scabs that covered most of my chest and both feet, and appeared to take on strange shapes. The largest one completely covered my right breast and looked like the map of Ireland; it even had a hole in it that looked like Lough Neagh in Northern Ireland to me. That and the one on my right arm were the biggest and stood about an inch proud of my skin, with the rest of them varying in size, shape and height. I also had a beauty right across my chin that itched like mad and never stopped oozing, as if it was constantly leaking.

But it was the smell that kept me awake at nights; that smell of burning flesh and particularly hair, which has never left me. It would come from nowhere and waft over my senses like a blanket covering me, causing me to stop whatever I was doing at the time and tense, as if I expected the ball of flame to pick me up and hurl me against a ditch again.

I was allowed to wear a pyjama bottom only (supplied by the hospital, since I had arrived completely naked) and I spent most of my time huddled under the cotton sheets shaking from the cold. During the night, when sleep finally arrived, the sheets would snag the scabs as I tossed and turned. Many a night I woke up covered in sweat, with the smiling face of a nurse bending over me, telling me that I was all right and I was only having a dream. Since the scabs were being plucked away with the assistance of the sheets, I would prise them up and peer under their hard, black, shell-like structures to view with growing interest the mounds of soft, pink skin that matched exactly the shape of the outer shell. Almost as if they were strangely shaped moulds that had been stuck to my body.

I learned all about pain during that first week in St James's – and I learned to live with it. As my own way of coping, whenever I was asked how I was feeling by the visiting doctor and his entourage, I always answered, 'Fine Doctor, when can I go home?' Otherwise, if I said I was hurting, a nurse would appear as if by magic and proceed to jab needles into me. Shortly after my arrival I had what they called a 'relapse', which had them all clustered around behind my curtain peering at me. They hadn't a clue what was wrong, so they rushed me down to the X-ray department again to photograph my chest, in the hope that it would give them some idea. But they needn't have bothered, as I could have told them myself what was wrong if I had felt inclined to do so –which I didn't.

I had woken up that same morning and decided that I had had enough: I wanted to die and for me it was a perfectly logical conclusion. I had had enough of the pain, hospital, injections, picking black scabs off my chest when I woke up in the mornings – and I had especially had enough of that bloody smell that just wouldn't go away. I had become selfish; I didn't think about what Catherine must be going through, holding on to life with a strength that I did not possess. Here I was, feeling sorry for myself, as if I was the only person in the world with a problem. So that morning I simply let go, with amazingly rapid results. It was as if after I had made the decision my body just said to itself, 'Thank Christ. He's finally quit fighting, now we can stop too and have a long and permanent, well-earned rest.'

The father and his two brothers turned up that same afternoon. This was one of the better visits of my stay in hospital, making me feel that perhaps dying wasn't the cleverest idea after all. They stood around my bed, the father on my left, Stan at the bed's end, and Tom over on my right, continually cracking jokes.

'What do you think, Stan; he's like you now, bald as a coot?'

'Well at least he'll catch the ladies' attention.'

'I don't know,' said Tom, 'I think that the alterations to his face have made him more handsome.'

'Well,' said the father, getting into the rhythm of things, 'look at all the money he'll save on razors for a while.'

On and on the banter went for at least an hour, and every word I uttered in a feeble attempt to match the teasing made them fall about laughing, as if it was the funniest thing they had ever heard. As they were leaving, with my spirits the highest they had been since the explosion, Stan turned, walked back to me and, patting me ever so gently on the head, said, 'You'll never have to worry about going to hell, lad, you've just come from there.'

After my relapse the parents called in to see me every evening on their way home from visiting Catherine, with whom they spent most of each day. And, while they tried to keep up a happy and jovial appearance, I could tell that things were not going well at St Vincent's, because the strain on the mother's face told a different story. This made their visits uncomfortable, since her body may have been in my ward, but her mind definitely was not.

Pride was one of my biggest problems. This was in spite of the fact that the father had pounded into my head, not so much by speech as by action, the idea that no matter how bad you felt, or if you were in a situation you didn't like, you never showed it outwardly. For me the worst thing about hospital was the indignity of the bedpan. I hated it: I felt that it sucked away any tiny shred of dignity that remained after being poked, prodded and inspected (as if I was some live 'specimen') by anybody in authority who was passing. And they especially watched you like a hawk to see if you did anything in the toilet department, because if you didn't they galloped up to you and poured some vile liquid down your throat. Which, when it kicked in, would tie up the bedpan for hours.

Now I had a small arse and, since the bedpans must have been modelled around someone whose rear had a 20-inch circumference, mine tended to fall into them. So I had hover over it, using the muscles in my back and upper legs to hold me up. There were some people who didn't care one iota and just sat there making all sorts of noises as they completed their task. At times they made so much noise that it sounded as if they were trying to start up an old tractor: all they needed to do was give themselves just a little more 'choke' and up they would start and run out of the room.

Not me. After a few days of what I considered gross humiliation, I requested that they permanently park a wheelchair alongside my bed. I could then drag myself into it and paddle my way to the bathrooms, which also gave me my first taste of freedom for some time, because I could zoom up and down the corridors and check out the rest of the wards.

According to the doctors, my upper body was mending itself nicely and, while I would carry the scars to my grave, I was told that they should (if I minded them for the next few years) present no future problems. It was my feet, and particularly my ankles, which had them a little perturbed, since it seemed that the tendons had been burned. So, not only could I not feel anything below the ankle-bone, but every time they stood me up I just fell over. And believe me (what with my eagerness to get away from the bedpan), I, more than anybody else, wanted to be able to walk again.

It was on the morning of the 7 October 1966, just seventeen days after the accident, that I first hauled myself into the wheelchair, backed into the toilet cubicle and, on finishing, stood up and walked back into the ward pushing the wheelchair in front of me. I could walk again, although not for long, as the pain from the blood rushing down my legs into my feet was nearly worse than the burns – but I could walk. This was also the day when I heard about Catherine. For the rest of the morning I sat on the edge of the bed watching the door and, at precisely ten minutes to noon, the parents arrived. They walked over to me and my mother said, 'You are all that we have left now, your sister died this morning.'

There three of us were, crying at one end of the public ward, while the other patients (conspicuously silent) tried to allow us what privacy they could. The mother produced a small, plastic box with a transparent cover, containing a lock of hair that she had cut off just after Catherine had slipped away. They had been with her throughout the night and, just before she finally gave up the fight to live, she had opened her eyes and smiled at them. Then she lifted her arms and, with an almost inaudible sigh as if it was a welcome release from the pain that she must have suffered, Catherine died as she had lived – causing no trouble. She left a void within the parents that would never be filled and would irrevocably change their lives.

As for me, when the parents left to make arrangements for her funeral, I didn't feel the same loss as they did. I knew that she would never leave me. If she had lived she would have spent the rest of her days in a wheelchair, with arms and hands that would never function properly. She would have lived, disfigured, in a society that would struggle to accept the bonny face belonging to a body that no man could find attractive. Catherine – a proud child, overflowing with so much life and laughter, whose spirit brought peace to all those with whom she came into contact – would not have wished for that existence. So, for me, she never died; for the rest of my life she would be with me as that four-year-old, mischievous sister, young forever.

Perhaps if my parents had not let their grief overwhelm them totally and had accepted Catherine's passing from this existence into a different and greater dimension, a place without pain and disfigurement, her death might eventually have brought them peace, both in themselves and with each other. And an understanding that tragedies are part of life. But it was not to be. However, as life goes on in spite of tragedy, so must this story . . .

A Taste of 'Compo'

I WAS TOLD that almost everyone in Inchicore turned out for Catherine's funeral. Her small, white coffin was taken from St Vincent's Hospital to St Michael's Church. They packed the aisles and the pews; they lined the streets on both sides from our shop to the church, and every business on Emmett Road closed that day as a mark of respect. It was said that her's was one of the saddest funerals ever to be held at St Michael's. Her little coffin was carried from the church to the hearse by the father and his brother Stan, to the slow rhythm of the bells beating out their mournful tattoo. The day was drizzling rain, which (it was suggested afterwards) was not rain but the angels crying; all that could be heard in the street was the subdued weeping of the people waiting to wish her a final farewell.

As the cortège wound its way through the streets of Dublin they blocked roads and halted traffic. They transported Catherine's remains to her final resting-place in Deans Grange Cemetery, where she was placed in a new plot over by the eastern wall of the graveyard. By the time I was shown her grave a statue of a kneeling angel had been erected, with her photograph inserted into its base. Engraved on a small and simple marble slab were the words 'Catherine, aged 4, tragically taken from her parents and brother, returned to the angels, 7th October 1966.'

My mother was present at her birth, my parents were there for her death and burial; I had missed it all, I had been saved pain and grief that probably only a mother could put into words. I have no idea how long I was in hospital after the funeral – a day, a week, a month – all I know is that one morning the specialist examined me and, turning to the sister who was hovering at his elbow, said, 'Sister, he can go home now, why is he still here?'

He repeated his words to me as if it was my fault that I was still occupying a bed, until I reminded him of my feet, which he had forgotten to examine. On checking them, he decided that perhaps I should stay on in the hospital for a bit longer. Getting my legs readjusted to walking again turned out to be a bigger problem than I had anticipated. I spent as long as I could bear banging up and down the corridor with the aid of what they called a 'walker', which I thought was a strange name for a gadget that you had to hump up and down in front of you. The pain that attacked me as soon I stood up was almost unbearable, pain caused by the rush of blood pumping down through unused and damaged leg muscle. Especially when the blood came to the ankles and rounded the corner towards the toes, setting the skin on fire, as if I had just stepped into a tub of boiling water. I had to stop every few paces and hold up first one leg, then the other, until the throbbing receded, before walking on another few steps. Repeating the process again and again, all the while dodging Molly, Mary, and all the other traffic pelting up and down the long corridor.

A few weeks later the same consultant and nursing sister finally announced that I could go home at last, then proceeded to give me a long list of what not to do. I was never again to go out in the sun uncovered, otherwise the scars would open up once more. I was to make sure I didn't scratch or cut them in any way, otherwise they might be re-infected and I would be back in hospital as their guest again. I had to treat my ankles with an antiseptic spray every night until my supply of four tins ran out. Little did he know that they would never run out, as I was sure that the dispensary had a fine stock of them.

I asked the nurse if she would please contact the dispensary where my father worked and somebody there would make sure my parents got the message. At around one o'clock that afternoon the district nurse from the dispensary arrived to collect me. Prior to the accident I could have been classed as thin, even very thin, as I was tall for my age. But now I was fat, very fat in fact. I had probably put on about four stone in weight. I was like a young Buddha and the only item of clothing that would fit me was a new pair of elasticised pyjamas that the nurse had brought with her, together with a pair of slippers and an overcoat.

It was only a short drive home: we came out by Rialto gate, down the South Circular, into Bulfin Road, and finally up Emmett Road. As we pulled up in front of the shop, which had not reopened yet, I was just in time to witness the father physically chucking the parish priest out of our hall door on to the pavement. Whatever small bit of religion the father had possessed prior to the accident he had lost completely when he carried Catherine's coffin to the grave. He now roared at the top of his voice to the retreating figure of the priest, 'What kind of fucking God do you represent that He can allow my daughter to be taken the way she was? Fuck off, and never come back to this house again.'

Quickly bundling me out of the car, the nurse took me straight upstairs to my old room, since the father had not noticed us and had retreated back inside without looking left or right. She put me into the bed that Catherine and I had often shared, and I lay there, listening to the hullabaloo going on downstairs in our kitchen. It sounded as if there was a great drinking session in progress. I remember at that moment feeling nothing: no pain, no emotions for Catherine's death, and especially no feelings in any way towards the parents. It was as if they had become complete strangers who were now acting as my official guardians. A light must have gone out inside my head, because the next few months became a blank. I simply have no recollection of my existence. When I look at a calendar, I can see that at some point during this time my eleventh birthday came and went, followed by Christmas and New Year's day. What I did know was that in our household there was never again going to be any singing or black-haired coal-bearer to celebrate the passing of the Old Year into the New. Drink was the only god now being worshipped, for every evening the parents took themselves across to the Workman's Club and drank themselves into a fighting state. Lying awake in my room, I could hear them leave the Club (along with the rest of the neighbourhood), already arguing with each other as they made the short journey across the street to our door. The slamming of the hall door had the same effect as the ringing of the bell in a boxing ring, announcing to the two combatants that they should 'come out fighting'. It was always the same alcohol-induced argument about who was responsible for Catherine's death – and it carried on into the small hours of the morning.

Sometime in January, my awareness reactivated, I woke up to a new word that was now taking over every conversation and being tossed about as if it were the new religion. The word was 'compensation'. It was to be our saviour, our new beginning; it would give us wealth beyond our imagination. It would allow us to start a new life without Catherine, in another place, where the memories of her life could finally fade into the background instead of reminding us daily of where she had sat, ate, played and slept.

The parents didn't set out with the 'compo' mentality; it was introduced to them one evening by Boy-o-Boy, who ranted on for over an hour about the recompense they were entitled to from the gas company who had gone and blown us up.

'Boy, oh boy, Ron, those bastards have ruined your life. Boy, oh boy, make them pay, pay dearly. Sue their arses to the wall. Boy, oh boy, Ron, get a good solicitor and get him on the case.'

And that is exactly what they did. Back then, for the parents and probably the majority of people in the country, suing somebody was a momentous undertaking. Also, although the father was street-wise, the mother was from country stock and had been brought up to believe that people were, in the main, honest, and that suing somebody was deceitful and unfair. As a matter of fact, she believed that suing was 'only for the poor', adding '. . . and what would the neighbours think of us, Ron?'

Within a week all the neighbours had their say in the matter, culminating in a good old drinking session in our kitchen, with Boy-o-Boy leading the proceedings from the kitchen sink where he was within easy reach of water for his whiskey.

'Boy, oh boy, Ron, I've being telling you for weeks that the capitalists in the gas company need taking down a peg or two.'

'He's right there, sure wasn't there another case, a week before your explosion, when a Calor gas bottle blew the roof off a house down the country?' This from old Coleman, sitting on a straight-backed chair in the centre of the room alongside the mother, whose head was swinging from side to side as if she was watching a tennis match as she followed the conversation around the room.

'There was nobody hurt in that blast, but I bet they got a pretty penny to fix up their house again,' said Klepto Joe. He had taken up position by the empty fireplace and was eyeing the mantelpiece, presumably wondering if he could fit the large glass ashtray, which the father had 'borrowed' from the Workman's Club, into his pocket.

The father, as yet, had not said anything throughout the evening as he stood with his back to the gas stove. He was a master at directing this type of discussion and, as long as he agreed with the direction in which the conversation was going, he would keep quiet. Then, when he thought the moment was right, he'd interject at the perfect time to reinforce his argument. He knew that a slip at the wrong moment could sway the mother against suing, which would have been detrimental to the father's plans. Waiting for a lull in the conversation he began.

'You'll never guess who I bumped into yesterday? Err, Joe, you probably know the fellow. It was that old shyster of a barrister who gets all of those criminals off in the Four Courts, Barrister Murphy, isn't it?'

Knowing the father, this was no chance meeting; but he had laid the seed and now all he needed was for Klepto Joe to take the bait: which he did.

'Christ Ron, I haven't seen that old bugger for years, I'm surprised he's still alive, especially with the amount of drink he consumes.' Joe held out his glass for a top-up, then continued reminiscing about Murphy, which was just what the father wanted him to do: tell a funny story, get everybody amused and slightly off the subject at hand. Before you knew it, we would be off suing the gas company with the mother's full consent.

∽

You would have thought that we were going to meet the President of Ireland, what with the hullabaloo the mother made about our impending visit to the solicitors. She dressed me up in my finery, and the father had to wear his 'burial suit'. On arrival at the blue Georgian door of their offices, we were ushered into a waiting-room that had a polished oak table in the centre, with a bunch of mismatched chairs surrounding it like old buttresses supporting the walls of a castle. The walls were lined with bookshelves that ran to the ceiling, and on the mantelpiece an old clock ticked away showing a time that must have been relevant to some other country in the world, as it had no bearing on Irish time.

In a short while I became bored and moved over to study the lines of books, accompanied by the mother's sharp, 'Now don't go and touch anything, do you hear?' While I was preoccupied, the mother and father conversed in whispers as if they were in church. After what must have been a good thirty minutes, the door crashed open and three solicitors stamped in. The eyes nearly jumped out of my head, as they were the spitting images of Curly, Larry and Mo from the Three Stooges, except they were dressed in identical dark suits as if they had gone out and bought a job lot together. When the father had made the appointment he must have also dropped off some details about what we were after. For no sooner had the mother settled herself into her seat and opened her mouth with the intention of speaking first, than the one who looked like Larry opened the file in front of him and cut her short. At which point the mother eyed the father, as if he should give out to the fellow for not allowing her the right to start off the proceedings.

'Well,' began Larry, 'we have reviewed the information that you gave us,' which had Curly and Mo nodding their heads in agreement, 'and we all concur,' more nodding from Curly and Mo, 'that you have a valid case against the gas company.'

The mother wiggled her rear end on the seat with excitement, the father smiled and nodded and I took the opportunity to replace the book that I had been hiding behind my back. The mother couldn't restrain herself any longer and blurted out the question, 'How much will we get?' Which caused the father to look at her disapprovingly. 'Difficult question, difficult question,' said Larry, glancing left and right trying to catch either Curly or Mo's eyes. But they were now both showing great interest in the ceiling.

'Er, without consulting with my two associates here,' Mo now began scratching himself somewhere on his person, under the table, 'I would be only guessing mind, but a case like this, well, let me see, somewhere in the region of forty to fifty.' Both Curly and Mo nodded their heads in agreement.

'Forty to fifty what?' asked the father in a very measured voice.

'Pounds I should say, not guineas, but,' he turned to Mo, 'didn't that judge last year award in guineas?' Mo screwed up his eyes as if trying to remember.

'Forty or fifty pounds compensation?' said the mother in a high squeaky voice.

'Ha, ha, ha, good lord, madam, no,' and he leant forward beaming at us. 'Thousands is what we mean, forty to fifty thousand pounds madam.'

There was a stunned silence from our end of the table and, for the first time in her life, even the mother was caught for words, as Larry continued, 'However, we have a lot of work to do; a case like this could take years before it reaches the court, so if we can now begin? Right Mr Heaps, once again, tell us exactly what happened, from the beginning.'

At that time this amount of money was a small fortune. So, in spite of the fact that we might be waiting years for the verdict, to celebrate our impending elevation in monetary status (and with the bank's assistance), the father promptly went off and retired the old Popular. He returned home with a brand new Ford Zephyr, which, in 1967, was the car of all cars. We were the envy of the street. The motor was the biggest I had ever seen: silver in colour, with the bonnet as big as a snooker table and front and back bench-seats large enough to hold a party on.

Even Boy-o-Boy was impressed when he dropped by one evening on his long way home. In spite of being in his customary drunken state he couldn't have missed it, for the father had parked the car on the pavement right outside our hall door.

'Boy, oh boy, Ron,' he began, even before he poured his first drink, 'did you know that some bowser has parked a bus right outside your front door? There should be a law about that kind of thing, cluttering up the entrances to hard-working people's homes. Boy, oh boy, it's not right that some eejit should own something as . . .'

At that point the father interjected before he went overboard, 'It's ok, it's mine, I've just bought it.'

Boy-o-Boy just stood there, shocked, like Lot's wife when she had been turned into a pillar of salt, transfixed, his mouth opening and closing without saying anything. Until eventually his brain caught up with the moving mouth and, sitting down and shaking his head from side to side, he mumbled, 'Boy, oh boy, Ron, but the "compo" came through right quick.'

∞

The father had been given a leave of absence from his job and I was not going back to school for the rest of that year. As the parents needed to get away from daily reminders of Catherine, it was decided that we would travel down to the mother's part

of the country where we could recuperate, while keeping an
eye on the pending court case.

All I can remember of those few months is two hotels that
we stayed in: one in Fermoy and the other in Youghal. The
parents spent most of their evenings in the residents' lounge,
telling everybody and anybody who would listen of the tragedy
that had befallen us. It always ended with me having to present
myself to complete strangers and show them the bright pink
scars that adorned my chest, while the mother broke down in
tears and the father went off to order another round of drinks.

I felt like a performing monkey that had to remain on
hand until beckoned over to expose itself – as if the sight of my
disfigurement would add credence to the story. I hated those
evenings and I began to detest the wallowing self-pity that the
effects of alcoholic overindulgence had on the parents.
Particularly the mother, who always began with the same
words, 'You know, I had tragedy', her eyes brimming over with
tears as if we were the only people in the world to have suffered
any calamity.

One evening the mother met a new lady in the bar and,
before long, out came the usual words, 'I've had tragedy, you
know.' The woman sat quietly and attentively throughout the
rendition, tears and all, and only interjected once to say, 'I am
so sorry, your poor thing, you must have gone through hell.'
When the mother had concluded her story, the woman began
to tell us her own tale.

She was from England and, earlier that year, every
member of her family had been wiped out in a car crash. Her
husband, two sons and one daughter – all gone, smashed to
pieces in one fell swoop. Now I thought that this was a pretty
horrific story and a lot worse than ours, but not the mother.
No, this woman's husband could be replaced and, as her
children had been years older than Catherine, their deaths

didn't have the same impact as that of a four-year-old.

No, no, that woman didn't know tragedy as well as the mother did.

Eventually I would be allowed to retreat back to my darkened room to await the arrival of my old tormentor, which I had now grown to accept as a permanent part of my life. Back would come the awful smell, filling the room with its rotten stink, and I would have to get up and open a window in a feeble attempt to rid the place of the smell of burning flesh and hair. It was always better when we stayed in Youghal, as we were close to the sea and during the night I could climb out of the window in my room and walk to the beach, gulping in the sea smells of salt water and seaweed, which acted as an antidote to the stench filling my nostrils.

The 'compo' claim wasn't going according to plan, since the gas company were putting up a good defence and still claimed that their bottle had not been the primary cause of the explosion. Their lawyers were making out that the father's Primus stove, with its deadly container of methylated spirits, had been nothing but a portable bomb that had exploded first and set off the gas cylinder. Not their fault at all, and nothing to do with them. Stranger still, the crucial piece of evidence (namely the gas bottle) seemed to have disappeared. Oops, what a shame, since it had 'only' been taken away for 'safe keeping'.

Over the next few months I became the main exhibit in the case, because our solicitors were forced to base all their evidence concerning the damage caused on my own carcass. They used maps and drawings of the area in which the caravan had stood and measured the distances between where Catherine had been lying, I had been sitting and the father's position when he had struck the match. In this way they hoped to present a case that would prove, without any doubt, that the Primus stove could not possibly have blown itself up, particularly since methylated spirits is a very low combustible fuel, incapable of going 'bang'. Gas had been leaking out of the cylinder for at least twenty-four hours before the accident, thus causing Catherine's death, although she had not been in the direct line of the fireball. The damage caused to the rest of the cul-de-sac (all of the surrounding trees and bushes had gone up in a cloud of smoke) was again due to the leaking gas that had settled there during the preceding day and night. The weather reports for that period proved that there hadn't been a breath of wind to disperse the gas that had collected near the caravan.

If I had thought that displaying my scars for all those drunks in hotels had been bad enough, I soon found out that it had been a mere prelude to the main act that followed. For the preparation of the court case I had to be examined by the specialists chosen by our solicitors. Skin, eyes, nose, ears, feet, chest and any other specialist that they could think of – I visited them all. It got to the stage where I could remove my clothes faster than a prostitute on a windy night in Phoenix Park. They prodded, poked, photographed, examined, tapped, stared and peered at every part of me, from the top of my head to my big toes. They made plans to remove skin from my thighs and transplant it onto my face and chest. They rigged me to a machine that nearly popped the eyeballs out of my head and, at the end of all of this, charged a fortune for every visit.

They all concluded that I had been in a gas explosion, since I could not have sustained my injuries in any other way. Well, I could have saved them a lot of time, as I was there when the cylinder went 'whoosh'. The only good news in this rigmarole was that I was still too young for them to carry out any of the repair work they were suggesting. 'Bring him back to us for the skin grafts when he has stopped growing and, by the way, here is our bill.' Which was always in guineas, never pounds. Pounds (the father patiently explained to me) are what you use to buy food and clothes, but guineas are what you pay to specialists or use to buy horses. I thought that the ordeal might be drawing to an end when we slammed the front door after the last specialist. But then the solicitors acting for the gas company (who up until then had been very quiet) finally announced their presence.

Now it was their turn to contradict the piles of medical reports regarding my condition. They wanted me to visit their own appointed specialists, just in case ours had made some mistakes in their findings. When visiting the specialists retained by the parents, I had always been ushered into rooms with my mother in tow, and she invariably did the talking, as if somehow I had been struck dumb. We were usually met by a dark-suited, smiling face, who would go 'hmmm', and 'I see', as I unveiled my framework. He would spend hours chatting to the mother while I stood in the middle of his well-appointed room, wondering whether to put on my clothes again. Or waited to be beckoned over to stand by his seated form, or waited to be told to lie on a brown leather, elevated examination table.

All in all, very civil altogether. If they weren't scaring the life out of me with their talk of operations (present and future), they bored me to death with their small talk.

'Hum, hum, can you please raise your right arm for me, there's a good boy.'

'Hum, hum, very good, very good', as if I had just performed a tremendous feat of gymnastics.

'Hum, hum, now Madam, if you look here you can see where the tissue over the right side of the chest has been very badly damaged, owing to the molecular structure of the . . .'

And so it would go on, as if they were discussing a lump

of meat that would fail to take a prize at next year's Royal Dublin Show food exhibition.

Not so with the gas solicitors' bunch. Although they had similar addresses and looked much the same, they treated me as if I was nothing short of a liar and as if, somehow or other, I must have inflicted the damage to my person on my own, while nobody was looking.

The opposition lawyers also went one better in the specialist line-up: they arranged for me to see a psychiatrist, which was the strangest interview that I had during the whole saga. He was a heavy, jolly-looking fellow, wearing a huge pair of glasses, so that when you looked into his eyes through his specs, he resembled an owl observing his prey. He even made me lie on his couch, just as you would see on TV.

'Well, young man, how are you feeling?' This in his rich, hypnotic voice that I was sure could lull me to sleep if I succumbed to it.

'Fine, fine.' I had learnt when I was in hospital that this was the best response to make; any other answer tended to have the nurse galloping over, quicker than you could blink, with the injection trolley bouncing and rattling in her wake.

'Good, good . . . any pain anywhere?' He raised his bushy eyebrows, which were magnified behind his glasses and looked like two rows of shaggy hedges.

'Eeer, no, I don't think so.' I thought this was another catch question.

'Good, gooooood . . . now would you like to tell me what happened?'

'Which bit?'

'Take me back to the accident, and what you remember in your own words. Now take your time.'

So I began, yet again, from the beginning. Where Catherine was lying, where the mother and father had been,

what the weather was like, how I saw this yellow fireball
coming towards me, how it lifted me into the ditch behind,
and how I ran down to the stream to quench the flames, and
. . . here he snapped to full awareness and interrupted me.

'So you weren't there when the explosion happened?' He
retrieved a note pad and pen from his inside pocket and began
to take notes.

'Of course I was, how do you think I got burned?' I
stopped myself just in the nick of time from adding 'you eejit'.

'But you said that you ran from the clearing?'

'Yes, but that was after I was hit by the fireball. I had to put
out the flames, so I ran to a river near the road.'

'So you didn't see your sister getting burned?'

'No.'

'Why didn't your parents help you, when you told them
you were on fire?'

'It all happened too quickly, the clearing was full of smoke
and fire, I just panicked and ran.'

'Did you see your father with the Primus stove?'

'Yes, I already told you, I saw him take it from the boot of
the car and set it up behind the gas cylinder.' This fool was
beginning to get me flustered; I had already told him all this.

'And you saw him strike a match?'

'Yes, I . . . saw . . . him . . . light . . . the . . . match.' I said
this slowly, just in case he was hard of hearing as well.

'So how are you so sure that it was the gas cylinder that
blew up, if all you saw was a yellow flame and then smoke?'

'I just know, that's all, sure it had to be that!'

Here he changed tack completely. 'Tell me how you feel
about your scars?'

Well, I had to admit this question stumped me, as, up
until that very moment, I hadn't really thought of them one
way or the other. All I knew was that they were there and

probably would be for the rest of my life. My mother had continually told me that, as I was a man, they really didn't matter; the only thing that any woman would look at would be my job prospects. I was to concentrate on getting a good education, going to university, and coming out with some qualification or other.

'Well, the doctors at the hospital told me that I can never go out in the sun again.'

'Does that bother you in any way?'

What sort of a question was that, at eleven years of age? I answered 'no'.

'Is there anything else that you would like to tell me about regarding the accident?'

'Well, . . . it's the smell.'

'What?' he roared, making me jump as well, 'What smell?' He must have thought I was referring to something in his chambers, as he began to look about the room as if I had spotted a dead rat on the floor.

'It's the smell of burning flesh and hair that I get every night, sometimes it gets so bad that I can't sleep.'

'Oh that,' he said, with relief evident in his voice, 'well, don't worry about it, as some reaction is bound to be expected.'

'But how do I get rid of it?'

'Well, don't worry, it will go soon, probably as soon as you start school again.'

And that was that, interview over. When we set out on the drive home and the parents asked me how it went, I replied that Dad was right, all psychiatrists were crackers and this fellow had been no exception.

Fire in the Hole

I WENT BACK to CUS in September 1967 to start a new school year. As I had missed out completely on the previous year's schooling, I thought I would be returning to Gleeson's class for another sentence. But the powers that be decided it would be better if I started year one of the secondary school and, if necessary, I could spend two years in that class before moving on.

I joined the Alpha lot (the 'thickos' of the school), along with about twenty-three others destined to spend the next six years together. This little group turned out, especially in our last two years, to be one of the most difficult classes that the Marist fathers had ever had to contend with. What did they expect? They treated us like fools, so as far as we were concerned we might as well act like fools, proving the old saying, 'If you dish out peanuts, well, expect a bunch of monkeys.'

We even had a different curriculum from the A 'geniuses'. For us there was to be no German, no physics, no biology and no chemistry (which was a pity, as Naty was still having difficulty in getting the sodium chlorate and sugar mixture to work). The biology they could keep, as I was not into cutting up frogs and dissecting rabbits. Anyhow, we were not being educated to go on to university. No higher English or maths

for us either. Over the next six years we were simply to be
taught the basics required for passing our Leaving Certificate.
If lucky, we could aspire to becoming bank tellers, or, if we
had the flair, draughtsmen or artists.

When I returned after my year-long absence, I was
waddling around a couple of stone overweight and had been
banned by the doctors from participating in any sport for at
least two years until the new scar tissue had completely formed.
Our solicitors encouraged this scenario because it would add
meat to the pending court case. I was sure they were also going
to suggest that I had been one of the school's up-and-coming
rugby stars.

The accident had done nothing to improve my spelling. If
anything it had become worse, and once more I found myself
up in front of the blackboard, chalk in hand, scribing down
what the teacher dictated. The level of humiliation was not
quite as bad as I had experienced over in the other building.
But the priest still found it necessary to remark to the class
that normally when they handed students over from across the
yard, the boys had been taught (at the very least) to read and
write. 'So, where oh where, dear Lord, did they go wrong with
you?'

The home front had settled down to quiet acceptance in
anticipation of our court case. But as I turned twelve we were
still facing another Christmas that none of us wanted to
endure. For some reason or another it had been decided that
we would spend Christmas Day in a convent, having dinner
with a bunch of nuns. I know that this was the mother's idea,
for the father (given a choice) would have spent the time in a
pub, far away from any nuns that reminded him of little girls
being abused. However, in spite of the father's strong
objections, to the nunnery we did go that Christmas morning.
Once there, we sat in a cavernous hall, at the longest table I

had ever seen, with the Reverend Mother about a mile away at the top being attended to by novices.

There was a prayer said between every course, which must have been a special show put on for us, since Catherine's name was mentioned fairly frequently. At three o'clock we waved goodbye to a group of nuns who had gathered at the main door to bid us farewell and returned to a cold house, where the parents installed themselves in front of the TV and promptly fell asleep. So ended Christmas Day in a household still mourning the death of a child that never could, or would, be replaced.

As the New Year slowly marched forward, I felt the house became rather like a dark cave. Once incarcerated in its gloomy interior a depression settled over all who dwelt within, only to disappear immediately you re-entered the daylight beckoning outside the hall door. The parents oscillated from silent depression, occasionally broken by the brief monotone sentences required to sustain any basic form of communication, to a fleeting, pre-accident rapport, exhibited when they returned from the pub nearly every evening. This good humour lasted only a short while, invariably ending with a shouting match as the alcohol levels pushed the start button that set off the 'accident-blame' syndrome.

If I misjudged their arrival time and was caught in the kitchen when they came back from the pub instead of being entrenched in my room, I would be subjected to a drunken period of the 'loving parents' game, in which they were delighted that I, at least, had been left to them. But we would quickly move on to the 'blame' game: I had been given the bike and, as a result of damaging my knee, I had been responsible for the whole disaster. When we reached this stage any attempt to go to bed was absolutely out of the question, because the accusations would follow me upstairs. I learned very quickly that I could only hope to see my bed by standing my ground and taking the abuse for a time. But inevitably there would be some word spat out that opened up my own emotional wounds and I would begin to fight back.

Finally, one or both of them would tire and retreated to their own room, leaving a silent, highly charged atmosphere in their wake that brought restless sleep. The next day the household would return to a quiet, stunned, temporary truce, as if the previous night's antagonism had somehow washed away the sorrow that they felt, like the intermission of a stage show that you knew would recommence very shortly.

I began to time my arrival home from school as late as I possibly could. Often I went with David to his house first, where we did our homework together and I was given slices of fresh bread spread thickly with bananas (my favourite) by his mother. Within a short period their home became my place of refuge, we became like brothers, and I was accepted into their household on that footing. I very rarely talked to David or his family about the pending court case. As far as I was concerned, it lay far in the future. Oh, the evenings dreaming with the parents about the new life that we were going to carve out for ourselves when we got the money were all very well. But, as the months went by, all their talk of court cases and compensation began to seem like the telling of a good fairy tale. With David and his family I lived in the here and now. Court cases and 'compo' were part of the mythical world that the parents had elected to live in.

The father was promoted (or at least that is what he called it) and moved from the dispensary in Inchicore to the head offices of the Eastern Health Board at St James's Gate, by the main entrance to the hospital. He was even given his own office, complete with secretary. He and his drinking buddies now spent their days commuting from office to pub, betting shop, back across the street to the office, and finally back to the pub again. Klepto Joe, was also a compulsive gambler and drinker and, as alcohol was the father's primary concern, their daily triple-cross wager on the horses was submitted as a sort of miracle speculation. Their principle was that if it did come up, they would treat it as bonus drinking money. They settled into a routine that suited them all: there would certainly always be someone across the street, within easy reach of the betting shop, to collect the day's winnings.

Coming home in the evenings, I would often find the mother in bed, which suited the father and me very well, since peace would reign downstairs provided we brought her evening meal up to her. This I was more than happy to do, because it kept the two of them apart and allowed the father to carry on drinking in the kitchen uninterrupted. However, sometimes, owing to too much alcohol, he would make a complete hash of the meal. If the results of a botched job were presented to her, she would be out of the bed and downstairs as fast as a rabid kangaroo, shouting and screaming at us – which rather defeated the purpose of cooking her a meal in the first place.

I believe that it was my mother's elder brother Matty who attempted to try and get us all back into some semblance of a family unit. Matty had a very large farm in county Cork and, along with his wife, Mary, was busy raising a family of eight: four boys and four girls. His eldest daughter, Pat, he sent to visit us in Dublin and she brought a friend with her, called Marigold. Their brief stay was like a visitation from two angels. They were both eighteen, lively, beautiful, and so full of energy and fun that the whole household was galvanised into feeling it wanted to join the land of the living again. They both had younger brothers at home and immediately adopted me. At the age of twelve I was ready to fall in love with the pair of them as if they were my older sisters. The parents also fell under their spell and laughter once again reverberated around the hollow walls of the house. Pending court cases and 'compo' were temporarily forgotten: the mother remembered she had a house to run and the father even sobered up, tickled by the idea of having two young ladies in tow.

As it was their first visit to Dublin, he and the mother introduced them to the local watering holes, as all good tour guides should. Nearly every evening the girls would collect me from school, endure the wolf whistles from the departing sixth-formers (with whom they were more than capable of dealing), and bring me to an early evening matinee.

The first picture they wanted to see (showing in a cinema just off Leeson Street) was *Romeo and Juliet*. I balked like a stubborn mule and refused to enter when I saw 'by William Shakespeare' plastered all over the posters at the entrance. The only way they could convince me that I would enjoy the film was by giving demonstration sword fights up and down the street, to give me a preview of the action. At the same time quoting lines from the play to each other, much to the amusement of everyone else. The onlookers in the queue must have had a hilarious wait, what with the sullen, fat boy standing as still as a rock in the middle of the theatre's entrance, while two lively ladies fought an imaginary sword fight around his bulk.

Their antics worked and, before I knew it, I was sitting between the two of them in front of the screen. Unfortunately after the first five minutes I spent the rest of the film cowering down behind the person in front of me, red in the face with embarrassment. Unable to look left or right in case one of them would see my glowing face, which must have resembled a flaming match. Mostly, I was embarrassed for the two girls, as I couldn't believe the attire that the male actors were wearing had passed the Irish Censorship Board. They had multicoloured, striped tights and they looked as if they had been poured into them; the effect was to magnify their private parts to the point at which they looked completely out of proportion with the rest of their bodies. As far as I was concerned, having elevated my new friends to a position of near sainthood, these two ladies should know nothing of the evil ways of men. And so I practically swooned when one of the actors uttered something along the lines of 'my cock is throbbing like a rooster'.

For this reason, aside from wondering whether Juliet's breasts would win the battle with her dress and eventually fall out and appreciating the theme music (which, to this day, floods me with nostalgia whenever I hear it being played), I remember practically nothing else of the film.

All too soon their visit came to an end. For a short time afterwards the energies with which they had infected the house lingered on. And before the environment could lapse back into its original state, a new drama began to unfold.

∽

'The nuns are coming home, the nuns are arriving.' The mother burst into the kitchen after reading a letter that had just come in the afternoon post from one of her sisters down the country.

The father promptly went across the street to the Workman's Club, while I hung around waiting for an explanation. Apparently, many years before I was born and while the mother was still in her teens, her two eldest sisters had been shipped of to a nunnery by their father, finishing up as teachers in a convent somewhere in the Australian outback. The last time the family had seen them was when they waved goodbye from a railway platform years before.

Now they were coming home for the first time. During their three-month visit (when the father heard the time span it promptly drove him back across the street to the pub) they were to stay a week with every brother and sister, including a week with us in Dublin. As it was thought that this would be their one and only trip, nothing was going to be spared to make them feel as comfortable as possible.

My mother had never lost her Cork accent during her years in England and Dublin, and had a loud voice that could carry across a 20-acre field – not only loudly enough for her to be clearly understood within the field, but with enough decibels left to carry a further 20 acres. She also had an annoying habit of saying 'what, what' in quick succession when you began a conversation, so a person would have to stop and restart the sentence.

When the nuns arrived we sat in the kitchen every evening after tea and waited for somebody to strike up a conversation. After day three of the visit the most obvious topics had been exhausted (there is only so much you can discuss with two nuns). However, the evenings continued to follow the same format. The mother would sit in one of our better, straight-backed chairs, as proud as punch that her two sisters were staying with us. The two nuns were installed in our only soft chairs alongside each other. The father sat on the edge of his chair, looking for any opportunity to bolt across the street – and then there was me, all dressed in my best school uniform, complete with school cap.

'Louvelely meeeal, Robert,' one of the nuns would finally comment in her soft Australian accent, as if she had been elected to become the spokesperson for the two of them.

'What, what?' the mother would roar, causing the nun sitting closest to her to jump with fright.

'She said it was a lovely meal.'

'What, what?'

'She said it was a lovely meal.' This time shouted to her by the father, which caused the other nun to jump in her chair.

More staring into space, as the mother had given an edict that on no account was the telly to be turned on, since it would be seen as the height of bad manners. A pity she hadn't consulted with her two sisters.

'Wheeen are we goooing to visssit Catherinnne's gravvvve, Robeeert?'

'What, what?'

'Tomorrow after lunch.' The father didn't bother to translate for the mother.

'What, what?'

To keep the peace, I now began to interpret and relayed messages until, inevitably, the mother turned to her sisters and requested that they sing that famous Australian song, 'Waltzing Matilda'.

'Oh no, not again,' I thought, as I watched the father excuse himself and make a beeline across the street, oblivious to oncoming traffic. As if on queue, the two sisters sang all one hundred verses of that damn song. If I never, for the rest of my days, hear another rendition of that song it will be too soon.

The whole of the mother's 'tribe', as the father referred to them, descended on our house for the farewell party. With one last rendition of 'Waltzing Matilda', with which the whole family joined in (by now they had all learned it off by heart), the nuns were waved off from Dublin airport with much wailing and tears.

'Ah Jesus, we will never see them again.'

'Bejesus, it might have been better if they had never come.'

'It's like they were dead, found, and now dead again.'

'The poor crators, flying halfway around the world to their

certain deaths.'

'Jesus, Matty, you shouldn't have left them go.'

'What do you mean, you rotten bastard, you're the eldest, you should have stopped them.'

And so it went on back at our house until the early hours of the morning. To date the two nuns have been back over six times and I do believe that another visit is imminent.

∞

I could never be described as a light sleeper; instead, my pattern of rest has been described as 'not sleeping, but taking a short course in death'. The rows at home began again, but this time with a difference. They were now starting up in the early hours of the morning. I would be brought rudely awake to the sound of my door crashing open, the light switched on, and I would then be hauled unceremoniously out of bed. After nursing geriatrics at St James's Hospital the mother had become quite adept at getting seemingly helpless people out of bed. She pulled back the covers, grabbed my feet, pivoted them over the edge of the bed, and, in one fluid movement, pushed down on my legs while hauling me up by the arms. The result was always the same: suddenly I was wide awake, standing upright in the middle of my room, totally disorientated, while she screamed at me, 'Listen to what your father is saying to me.'

This mystified me, as the father would be nowhere in sight but, dragging me by the hands, she would haul me out into the hall where she would continue shouting at their closed bedroom door.

'Come out here and tell your son on what you just said, you bastard.'

I would then be led into their room where the father

would be standing over in the corner, in his striped pyjamas, seething with barely controlled temper. His face contorted and his whole body trembling as if under tremendous physical restraint like a coiled spring ready to snap back.

At the time I could not understand the problem, but as I got older I came to realise why the mother dragged me out of bed in the early hours of the morning. It was her only protection against the father's sexual advances, as he wanted them to try and have another daughter to replace Catherine. However, at that time, I was totally ignorant of the situation and my only thought was, why am I standing here, freezing in the middle of a room, listening to yet another row? Now I had another horror to contend with as I lay in bed, the room in darkness, listening to the traffic and the voices of pedestrians passing outside. The smell of burned flesh and hair I had begun to accept as a part of my life, along with the physical reminder of the scars that I bore. A reminder that I had often shared this bed with Catherine. Only now, to add to this, I dreaded the fact that I might close my eyes to try and get some sort of rest – and then, bang, suddenly find myself standing in my room, right smack in the middle of a row.

Eventually I learned to tell by the sound of their steps on the stairs and the level of communication between them if the night would bring restful slumber or aggression. They were using me as a device to inflict pain on each other, and I was beginning to hate them. I plotted to escape from this environment and rebelled in every thought and deed against their wishes and instructions. To me, they had both lost their right to command me in any way.

I had just turned thirteen when, arriving home from school one evening, I found the father standing in the middle of the kitchen. He told me that my mother had been admitted into a nursing home in Dún Laoghaire and that he was closing the shop for good. Apparently the date of the court case had been fixed for the coming week, but that morning they had received a letter from our solicitors stating that it had been delayed until further notice.

I didn't know whether to feel elation or disappointment. Elation, because with the mother gone there would at least be tranquil nights. Or disappointment that the court case had been delayed until God only knew when – and what would we do for Christmas, which was only a few weeks away? I settled on elation, concluding that at least peace would reign under our roof for a while. We had our Christmas dinner in St James's Hospital, in the staff canteen, along with all of the other people on duty that day.

The father was now able to drink at his own discretion and spent most of his evenings across in the Workman's Club, so I learned to cook for myself.

Visits to the mother were regimented affairs, in which I stuck my head into the private room, said 'hello', and then departed as quickly as I could. That left the pair of them talking to each other about any new correspondence from our lawyers as if they were complete strangers who had just met for the first time and were discussing some mutual business deal.

I can't say that my schooling suffered, as the fear of being hauled up for the 'usual six' kept me in line with my studies, but since I was alone for many an evening I often rushed quickly through my homework. On the weekends I met up with Naty, who was still experimenting with things that could go 'bang' in the middle of the night. He had cracked the sodium chlorate and sugar mix, and so we spent many a Saturday evening preparing our explosive devices.

We used empty tablet tins with screw-on lids that I acquired from the dispensary when nobody was looking. They proved to be excellent containers for our experiments and so, once again, Emmett Road reverberated to the sound of explosions that kept the local gardaí baffled for months. We would drill a hole just slightly larger than the width of a drinking straw in the top of the tin, pack the tin with about a pound of our lethal mixture, and then screw the lid back on. Filling an ordinary straw with the same combination, we'd poke it through the hole so that it acted as a fuse. Then we picked a quiet location somewhere along the street where we would be undisturbed and, after lighting the fuse (which took a good minute to burn down), we'd retreat to a safe distance and wait for the big bang.

We were trying to think of new and interesting testing grounds when we remembered the Workman's Club and the carnage that we had caused with the bangers in the toilets. What could we do with this new power that we now possessed? The new toilets at the club had a flat roof that was easy to climb on to. The sewerage pipes for the toilets were made of 4-inch ductile iron pipe, all surface-mounted, and they ran up, down, sideways, and every which way on the back walls of the building, resembling a plumber's nightmare. However, there was one vent pipe, which stuck high in the air above the flat roof and, by standing on a bunch of empty beer crates, we could just about reach it.

Now we had a plan. One good charge thrown down the vent pipe, especially the iron pipes at the club, would reverberate around the whole building without causing any damage, and we thought nobody would ever figure out what had happened, because it would detonate in the sewerage pipes.

We picked the following Saturday night when the place was packed to the rafters. The whole operation took us less than five minutes: we climbed up onto the roof and dropped our fizzling tin into the vent pipe, where it clattered its way down until it lodged in one of the main sewerage pipes that ran off at a right angle. Throwing the crates back off the roof into the club's storage yard, we climbed back down again and, since we had doubled the length of the fuse, we had plenty of time to return to the safety of Naty's backyard before the device exploded.

It took longer than we had figured, but just when we had given up hope, thinking that the fuse must have gone out, off it went with a roar like an express train hammering through a narrow tunnel. Purely out of ignorance, we had not made any allowance for the fact that the vent pipe was full of methane gas. NASA would have been proud of the shot of flame that rocketed out from the top of the pipe and went a good 50 feet into the night sky, sounding like a thunderclap. Momentarily, it turned night into day and lit up the whole area, as if the Workman's Club was trying to join in the race for space supremacy against the Russians and the United States. Delighted with our night's work, as we had caused a bit of noise and plenty of flame, we went off for our usual bag of chips.

The next morning the father, who had been enjoying himself in the club when we dropped our charge down the pipe, warned me not to attempt anything as stupid as that again – if, as he suspected, we were responsible for the explosion. We weren't plumbers, so how were we to know that every single waste pipe inside the building was also connected to the 4-inch sewerage pipes? But we had been quite correct in our assessment that the place was packed. Apparently at the time of detonation it sounded to most of the clientele as if a 21A bus had hit the side of the building, head on. Others thought that the gas mains had gone up and ran into the toilets for protection – which, in hindsight, was a bad move on their part.

The thick-walled ductile iron pipes had contained the force of the explosion, but the energy created still had to go somewhere – and it did. It shot out of every waste pipe inside the building: toilet bowls, wash-hand basins and bar sinks. Forcing out, at great speed, any water or items lodged between the point of detonation and the escape route. Luckily nobody had been sitting on any of the toilet bowls at the time, as the force blew waste water, soggy toilet paper and lumps of shit all over the bathrooms, causing the toilet seats to jump up and down as if possessed by an evil spirit. The same happened with the wash-hand basins, although not quite to the same extent. But the worst confusion occurred in the main bar itself.

All of the large sinks were already filled with hot water, in preparation for the washing and rinsing of the hundreds of pint glasses used throughout the evening. The percussion blasted sink plugs and water up to the ceiling before showering down again onto anybody within range. Since nobody knew what was happening, bedlam reigned. But at least their plumbing pipes were given a good clean out and, in due course, the blame for the totally mystifying events was placed firmly at the door of the Dublin Corporation.

∞

I suppose everybody experiences certain turning points in their lifetime and, God only knows, I have been through a whole string of them. One of the most fortunate was triggered by my mother's brother Matty. On one of his visits to our house in Dublin he suggested to my mother that I should be sent down to his family farm for the summer holidays. This was to be my first introduction to a household that embraced me immediately as one of its own and gave me an insight into how wonderful family life could really be. My relationship with

Matty's family lasted for a number of years. They gave me new definition for the idea of family unity, which assisted me greatly in surviving the middle years of my teens without turning into a full-scale Dublin gurrier.

'Boulta', as the house and farm was called, comprised some 480 acres of prime agricultural land in the heart of east Cork, about 30 miles from the city. The house was a three-storey structure and dated back to the eighteenth century, with the later addition of two long, single-storey buildings that were used as the kitchen and informal dining-room. The first and second floors held two large bedrooms apiece, with my uncle and aunt on the first floor and the 'lads' (being Gerard, Noel and me) installed on the top floor. From its front windows our room offered a majestic view out over the front lawn and the ancient, oak-lined driveway that wound its way down to the main road. Looking left, I could see over the wall that marked the lawn boundary onto the slate roofs of the farmyard, with its long, low cowhouses, milking parlour, hay barn and stables for the herds of horses that appeared to roam everywhere at will. Over to my right, I was able to look down on the orchard where apple trees, tall in their own right, seemed dwarfed by the giant oaks that guarded the house.

In the distance I could see some of the farm's fields running down to the main road, which wound back up and out of sight behind the house. Dotted along the roadside were small cottages that I was told belonged to their tenants, with the menfolk employed on the farm and some of the women working in the house. It all gave me the impression that I had landed on some present-day gentleman's country estate. But for the two lads and me there was to be no idleness, since Matty had us up the next morning at eight to begin the day's farm work.

There was hay to be cut, turned, baled, stacked and, as the

final task, brought in and stored for winter feed in the hay barns. They had a large dairy herd of Friesians that required milking twice a day during the summer months. This mundane task was performed by one of their tenants who, on the very first day that I introduced myself to him, scuttled away fearfully as soon as I came within talking distance. Later on, during the course of the day, he dragged Noel and Gerard aside and warned them to keep an eye on me, as I looked like 'one of them Dublin gurriers' he had read about in the papers. He added that they had best keep a watchful eye on me, because I might draw a knife on them, or murder the whole family while they slept.

As for him, well, he wasn't going to let me near him in case I assaulted him in their stead. Amazing, the ideas that some of the older country folk harboured about 'Dubs'. If he had only known what the average Dubliner thought about 'culchies'; most hadn't a clue as to the origin of their daily food.

'Aagh, sure, Jesus, milk, what? Sure that comes out of a bleeden' bottle and me potatoes and cabbage comes from the grocer at the corner of me street. Those farmers don't do nottin' all day long except go to bleeden' funerals and to the pubs afterwards, what?'

Within a week I was driving a tractor, a Fordson Major, complete with power take-off. (Whatever that meant, but I knew it would sound great when I recounted to David what I had done on the farm.) In glorious sunshine days, we baled hay, with Noel operating the baler. Gerard and myself walked behind, standing the bales against each other in groups of four so they could dry out fully, with constant reminders from Noel to 'remember, knots down and out'.

Every morning Matty would explain his wishes regarding the day's work. Some days left us with plenty of time to explore the countryside, but when there was work to be done it came first.

Within a few weeks I began to regain all my old fitness and whatever hospital fat I had left was quickly replaced by muscle. The good food and sunshine acted like a tonic and the bits of me that were exposed to the sun turned golden brown in colour. After a day's work or play sleep came easily and, under Matty's roof, I was (for the first time in many a year) enjoying a good night's rest without the worry of being dragged out of bed to listen to the parents fighting. Even the remembered smell abated for a while. And, when it did come, it washed over me and passed on quickly, as if in gentle reminder that it had not gone away completely but was simply allowing me a restful break from the memory.

One particular Saturday evening Matty announced that he was going to take us to the pictures in Youghal. Straight after tea we all loaded into the Morris Oxford – Matty, Gerard, Noel and myself – and headed off, making a slight detour along the way. For some unexplained reason we called into Marigold's house and collected her younger brother and sister. A quiet, withdrawn girl climbed into the front seat along with her seven-year-old brother, leaving the three of us in the back. *The Good, the Bad and the Ugly* was showing to a nearly empty theatre, allowing us to spread ourselves out among the seats. At some point in the course of the picture the girl, who was sitting in the seat directly in front of mine, got up to take her brother to the toilet. I watched her lead him by the hand out through the double doors, and then something happened inside me and I experienced a feeling that was totally new to me. It was like a floodgate opening and discharging a mixture of giddiness and light-heartedness that caused my breath to come in short gasps.

All the way home I was mesmerised by her profile as she

sat staring out of the passenger window, as if concentrating on some object that only she herself could see. I don't think I heard her speak two words throughout the evening, so I had no idea what her voice sounded like. All I knew, by the time we dropped them back to their house, was that her name was Gina; she was eleven and I was thirteen.

The next morning Matty received a rare phone call from the father. He was to send me home straight away as, finally, we were going to court.

Judgement Day

OUR 'DAY IN the sun' had finally arrived. We were going to court; we were going to have our justice. The excitement and trepidation was almost palpable around the house as we prepared to leave for the Four Courts on the first morning of the hearing. The mother was shouting and screaming at the father and me, her normal behaviour when she was excited or worried; behaviour that we always had to bear in silence. At times like these I often wondered why the father hadn't told her to shut up and behave years ago. During the drive from Emmett Road to the quays her constant giving-out was nearly impossible to put up with. Nothing was right: I was dressed incorrectly, my shoes weren't polished enough, my hair wasn't combed properly, the father was driving too fast, the car smelt of cigarette smoke and he was not listening to her.

By the time we arrived at the courthouse they were both sulking and neither was talking to the other. I realised this particular bout of bad temper was due to the prolonged frustration they were experiencing, since the court case had been deferred by the Calor Gas solicitors for what had seemed like an eternity. During that time offers of compensation had been suggested to our solicitors, but these were always treated as ridiculous and rejected out of hand by both the parents and our legal advisors.

But now we had them. Justice would prevail. We were finally bringing them to the Four Courts, by the Liffey in Dublin, in High Court Room 3. We were going to nail them to the wall, given the sums of money that were tossed about by our solicitors and the parents; at that time, those figures were only seen in connection with the Irish Hospitals' Sweepstake.

As we ascended the steps leading into the main hallway, it seemed to me as if we were entering a Roman temple. My jaw dropped at the sight of the ornate floor and walls, the dome-shaped ceiling, and the sturdy pillars (whose shoulders appeared to bear the weight of the building) standing as guards. Pacing back and forth across the entrance was Larry, one of our solicitors. As soon as he spotted us he ran over and shook the parents' hands as if they were long-lost relatives, returning after years of enforced emigration.

I had been dressed up for the occasion in my school uniform and given the usual instruction to be 'seen, but not heard, unless spoken to'. Both my parents were dressed in dark clothing that blended well with the sombre mood the occasion seemed to demand, and also coordinated with the black gowns of our barristers. As we stood outside the courtroom waiting to be called in at the appointed hour, we made up a sizeable group, which included the parents and me, Larry, Curly and Mo, two barristers I had never seen before, plus various clerks and their henchmen. If the case were to be awarded on mob size, we would have won hands down. The opposition were assembled over in the far corner of the main hall and had an equal number of white wigs, but failed miserably with their gathering of hangers-on. They were speaking in hushed voices amongst themselves, and kept glancing over in our direction.

Finally a head popped out through the double doors and announced that we had five minutes left to go, which accelerated the final instructions being given to the father who was due to be the first witness on the stand. We all trooped in together, and the parents and I were asked to sit in the public seats immediately behind the partition separating us from the 'arena'. Then, with much straightening of wigs and flapping of black capes, our own team and the opposition forces filled every other available table and chair.

'All rise. His Most Gracious Highness, the Right Honourable Lord So-and-So is now presiding.' This was not, of course, what was actually said, but the court clerk might just as well have said that, for the person who walked out of a door leading to the judge's platform was dressed like a king. He wore a brilliant red robe adorned with tassels and dangling bits, and, precariously balanced on the top of his large head, was a tiny, off-white wig that matched his hair. With steel-rimmed glasses perched on the nose of a round face that expressed sternness bordering on hostility, he surveyed the array of his subjects drawn up before him. These 'subjects' bowed low, their stooped shoulders implying surrender before they had even begun. Then he gave a barely perceptible nod in the general direction of the public area and settled himself in his high-backed chair before motioning to the court clerk, who sprang up and handed him a pile of papers.

Although we were sitting directly behind our barristers, I found it very hard to hear what they were saying, since everyone spoke in hushed voices to the judge, now engrossed in the papers that the court clerk had given him. The only way I could tell when anybody was addressing the judge was when he or she stood up; from my perspective it looked like they were involved in a badly run game of 'musical chairs'.

No sooner would one of our barristers sit down than one of the opponents' would jump up. This gave our lot time to turn around and whisper to one of our solicitors, who appeared to be supplying the relevant information and

questions. I looked around, in vain, trying to figure out where
the jury was hiding, for surely you couldn't hold a court case
without them? I was just about to whisper this question to the
father, when suddenly everybody sprang up, closed his or her
books and bowed, just as the magistrate withdrew through his
back door like a magician performing a disappearing trick.
Apparently lunchtime had arrived, although it seemed to me
that we had only just started. I began to realise that this lot
had never heard of a 40-hour week. That first afternoon went
much the same as the morning: an hour and a half after we
had all trooped back in for the session, the court was
adjourned until the following morning.

'Well, I think that went well,' said the head wig to the
father, once we had gathered around him in the main hall.
'Not my best choice of judge for a case like this,' he continued,
'I'm sure he fell asleep during the afternoon session, what
George?' This last statement he addressed to his associate.

I strolled off to have a good look around, leaving them to
it because they were again discussing the father's testimony,
which they were certain would be given on the morrow. So far
I had found the whole experience quite amazing. Mainly
because there was no jury: no sign of twelve working men of
truth, no honest and upstanding brotherhood to hear our case
and award in our favour. No, the outcome of the case was
going to rest solely on the judge's discretion. So it went
without saying that we all had to be nice to him, and all I could
hope for was that the mother wouldn't abuse him over
something or other.

Of course that evening after we arrived home our kitchen
became the nerve centre: all the usual callers turned up to find
out how our first day in court had gone. After they had settled
themselves down with a drink, the father began, 'We arrived
at a quarter to eleven, to be met by our mob plus the gas

company shysters, resembling black vultures circling a trapped and dying animal, eyeing us from a distance. At eleven the court clerk called us in and they all began talking to the old judge who looked like he had spent the night in a brothel.'

'Did you get to wave at the jury?' broke in Not-My-Round Jim.

'There wasn't one,' said the mother in a voice that suggested that it was the father's fault. Well, that had them all babbling, talking at once, everybody ignoring each other in an attempt to voice an opinion on the matter and at the same time reaching for more drink. Finally Boy-o-Boy was able to get his view across, mostly due to the fact that he dropped his glass on the floor where it smashed into a thousand pieces and stunned the rest into silence.

'Boy, oh boy, Ron, call for a mistrial.'

'How can he call for a mistrial when it has only just started?' said Money-Lending Jim, who was one of the new acquaintances that the father had dragged back with him from the pub. (His nickname was a result of his wife's illegal business activities, lending money to destitute women at exorbitant interest rates.)

'How can you even call it a trial when there's no jury?' put in another of the new arrivals.

And so they went on, arguing long into the evening about the absence of a jury, about the judge, how much the barristers were costing, how long the case would go on for, were our lot going to be any good, and how much would the judge award us anyway?

The next morning found us back in the same courtroom and it looked like we were in for the same legal gibberish as the previous day until, with a flurry of activity and a straightening of wigs, the father was called to the stand to give evidence. As he got up, the mother grabbed my hand as if we were watching

him being led to the guillotine. No sooner had the father taken
two steps forward than the old judge looked at a large old clock
hanging at the rear of the room and announced to all that it
was, in fact, lunchtime and he would hear the evidence after
he had dined.

As soon as the court reconvened the father was called to
the stand where, in a clear and firm voice, he apprised the old
judge of the events leading up to and after the explosion.
Gradually a hushed silence descended over the courtroom as
the judge and barristers alike began to pay attention and
became fascinated with the account. The mother cried all the
way through his rendition, especially when he spoke of the
hours leading up to Catherine's death. Of how, on her last
day, they had sat through the night with her, holding her hand
and knowing she was dying, yet somehow hoping that their
presence would encourage Catherine to hold on to the tiny
spark of life that was slowly and quietly flickering away. And of
the way in which, on 7 October at 8.45 in the morning,
Catherine had opened her eyes, held out her arms towards the
ceiling, smiled at both of her parents and, with a final, peaceful
exhalation of breath, had died. Reaching into his jacket
pocket, the father then extracted a small, flat, plastic box with
a transparent cover and held it up, saying, 'This is all we have
left of our daughter, it is a lock of her light brown hair that my
wife cut the moment after she had left us.'

Pausing for a second as he slowly replaced the box in one
of his pockets, he went on to recount the details of Catherine's
funeral and the devastating effect it had had on our family.
The father, standing erect and straight-backed in the witness
box, with his hands gripping the smooth and well-polished
handrail, told his story not as if he was looking for sympathy,
but simply as a statement of the facts. He was never a person
to solicit pity or commiseration from anybody – and he

especially did not want it from that courtroom.

As he stared straight ahead, wearing the same suit he had worn to his daughter's funeral, it was as if he was peering at a giant TV screen at the back of the court that was showing a replay of the day he had carried Catherine's white coffin from the church to the graveyard. His voice never wavered as he concluded his testimony by commenting that, as a result of the accident, when they had reopened the shop it had never returned to any of its former glory.

The judge, who had been leaning forward with his elbows on his desk and his hands cupped in front of his lips while the father had been talking, broke the deep silence that had settled over his court with a polite cough and thanked him for his testimony. As he replaced his glasses on his nose, he informed everyone that the defence could put their questions to the witness the following morning. Then, before the court clerk could bawl out the usual 'All rise', the old judge disappeared through his back door as if he was suffering from a bad dose of the runs.

On leaving the court we were told by our lot that, all in all, the day had gone well for us. They especially liked the way the father had conducted himself on the stand, as they felt that his simple, truthful and accurate account had gone down very well with the judge. Mo even had encouraging words to say as we all went down the steps together: 'After today's account, don't worry about tomorrow, as I don't think that they can shake or rock your description of the events. Good night all, we'll see you bright and early in the morning.' Which, to them, meant any time after 10.30 in the day.

However, the next morning, after the father had again taken the stand, the defence team came straight into the attack without any polite preamble and put forward their head barrister for their opening barrage. He was a short, dumpy fellow in his mid- to late-fifties. I think we all took an instant dislike to him, as he had a face that a pedigree bulldog would have been proud to display, a characteristic that immediately earned him the nickname 'Bulldog' from the father.

'Yesterday, Mr Heaps, you told the court (and I quote) that you had just, a few days before, bought the replacement gas bottle from a local supplier and ferried it back to the caravan in the boot of your car.'

'Yes,' replied the father in a loud, clear voice. He had been warned not to elaborate on any of his answers and to keep his replies short and to the point.

'Can you please describe, for the court, the boot of your car, err . . .' (here Bulldog made a show of placing glasses on his nose and reading from a sheet of crumpled paper that he had obviously being carrying around in his pocket) '. . . a Ford Popular I believe?'

'Why?'

Well, that got him. Even the old judge smiled at that response, and Bulldog sniffed the air, as if he had just sensed a bitch on heat seven streets away.

'You placed a gas bottle, which you have claimed was faulty, in the back of you car. I just want to know if there was anything in the boot of your car that could have damaged it in some way?'

'Err . . . let me think . . . no.'

'Come, come, Mr Heaps, are you telling us that there was nothing in the boot of your car?' As his voice went up a few octaves.

'No.'

If he had started out with the intention of trying to rile the father, he was backing the wrong horse. Exasperated, he threw his hands in the air and turned to the judge.

'Ma Lud,' (his cheeks were flapping up and down now,

and beginning to turn red), 'will you please instruct the witness to answer the question?'

At which the judge turned to the father and smiled, twirling his glasses in his hands, and said, 'Mr Heaps, to satisfy my learned colleague, will you please tell the court what was in the boot of your car, as I am also at a loss and now curious, I might add, to see where this question is leading.'

The father responded with such an expression of mock horror on his face that it was a performance worthy of an Oscar. 'Ma Lud, I am terribly sorry, I understood that the question directed at me was in relation to anything in the boot of my car that could have damaged the gas bottle. Well, of course I answered "no". But as to the contents of the boot, well . . . let me think. Spare tyre, jack, wheel brace, some old newspapers, the Primus stove, a football, fishing-rod, golfing umbrella and . . . yes, I do believe an old pair of white underpants of mine that I left there to be used as swimming trunks in an emergency.' And he beamed at the barrister who had asked him the question as if he had just explained Einstein's theory of relativity.

Hell hath no fury like a woman scorned – or a pissed-off barrister made to look like a fool in front of his peers. The exchange now turned into a chess match between two masters, move and counter-move, until the judge finally called lunch, which came as a welcome relief to the two mentally exhausted sparring partners.

After lunch, as soon as the father took the stand, Bulldog stood up and waited a good minute before saying a word. Standing with his head bowed, he gave the impression that he was contemplating deeply what he was going to say next and when he finally spoke there was an audible sigh of relief from his colleagues.

'Mr Heaps,' he said, in a soft voice that bespoke unlimited

patience and even hinted an attempt at humour, 'a spare tyre, jack, wheel brace, old newspapers, a Primus stove, a football, fishing-rod, golfing umbrella, and old, white underpants of your own – an interesting collection of articles. However, you would have had to lay the gas bottle on its side, as the boot of a Ford Popular does not have enough room to place the bottle upright without leaving the boot open. Is that correct?'

'Yes.'

'So, as you drove back to the caravan site, the bottle could have been rolling back and forth in the boot?'

'No, because I wedged it in the corner with the umbrella.'

'Come, come, Mr Heaps, the bottle could have broken free and rolled all over the place.'

'It could have, but it did not.'

At this point Bulldog changed tack completely and asked, 'Do you know the weight of a refilled gas bottle?'

'Not offhand . . . no,' replied the father.

'Sixty-five pounds, or so I am reliably informed by the gas company. Now I put it to you, 65 pounds is a lot of weight. Suppose the gas bottle did, in fact, roll around in the boot as you drove home and, as you rounded a corner, it smashed into the Primus stove that you have already testified was in the boot of your car with such force that it fatally damaged it. So much so, that when you lit it on the day of the accident, it exploded.

'Look I have already told y . . .'

The Bulldog cut across him with 'no more questions Ma Lud'; he left the father simmering.

∞

During the next few days the Calor Gas defence council called on a whole bunch of other witnesses. Some I recognised as doctors I had visited, and some I didn't. They brought them

up from Ardkeen Hospital in Waterford – and the only reason
I could deduce for their appearance was to testify that we were,
in fact, the people that had arrived, burned, at their door that
day. The police, who had inspected the cul-de-sac after the
accident, gave a very good and precise account of the state in
which they had found the clearing when they arrived on the
scene, and described the immediate area as being badly
scorched and blackened. Of the foam mattress on which
Catherine had been lying, the only piece that remained was
the long zip that held on the dust cover. The base of the crate
on which I had been sitting had melted, along with most of the
tar on the old road.

When questioned by our side, the police confirmed that,
on arrival in the cul-de-sac, they had noticed that the gas bottle
had been blown into the ditch closest to the caravan door.
They also confirmed that they had removed everything they
thought relevant as evidence, and had stored the gas bottle in
the back of their police station. However, they couldn't explain
what had happened to the gas bottle, only saying that,
somehow or other, it had gone 'missing'. I thought our lot
would go berserk about the 'missing' gas bottle as it was a
major piece of evidence in our case, but, much to my disbelief,
they didn't. The only comment our white wig made was to say
'that is unfortunate'.

At the end of the day the father tackled Curly, Larry and
Mo with regard to the missing gas bottle. He insisted that the
next morning our white wigs drag the police back onto the
stand and demand a full explanation for the disappearance of
key evidence from the backyard of a Garda station. He finished
by saying, 'I'll tell you what happened. That flatfoot in there
left the gas company representative just walk in and take it.
The whole lot of them are in cahoots, I'll get the press down
here and tell them my side of the story.'

Larry calmed the father down by explaining, 'Attacking the Garda will not get us any brownie points with the judge. Anyway, at this stage, it is not that critical as we are a long way towards proving to the judge, without a shadow of a doubt, that it had to have been the faulty gas bottle that caused the explosion.' Patting the father on the back, Larry concluded by saying, 'Don't worry, leave us do our job'; and with that the three stooges disappeared off up the quays.

Arriving the following morning, we found all the barristers huddled together, theirs and ours, until eventually our lot broke away and, drawing the mother and father aside, began talking in frantic whispers. From what I could gather the gas company had made another offer. To my parents it seemed ludicrously low, but for some reason our wigs were advising them to consider it, as they appeared to be worried about something that for the moment they were keeping to themselves. The father stormed off in a temper, telling them to convey a message back to Calor Gas: namely, 'Go to hell.'

All through the court case they considered whether or not to put me on the stand, leaving me in a perpetual state of panic. The last thing I wanted was to have Bulldog tear into me, as I was positive that by the time he had finished with me I would be so confused I might even doubt that I had been there in the first place. To my utmost relief they finally decided against it and left the gas company to continue having their bash at refuting the evidence given.

The Primus stove had reappeared as their 'exhibit number one': amazingly the police had been able to look after that piece of evidence, but not our disappearing gas bottle. The father was recalled to the stand, where he was reminded that he was still under oath and asked to confirm that it was his. For the rest of that day we listened to various 'experts' for the defence discussing the hypothetical process by which the

Primus stove might have ignited and burned through the rubber hose connecting the gas bottle to the caravan, thus releasing the gas. Every time Bulldog, through his 'experts', tried to suggest this as a probable cause for the explosion, one of our white wigs would hop up and ask the so-called expert to explain, given this scenario, how the mattress on which Catherine had being lying could possibly have erupted in a sea of flames. Or what had caused the tar on the road to ignite and melt if the gas in the bottle had not been leaking for some time?

At the end of that day another offer was made to the parents, but whatever was said to the father resulted in him turning, without a reply, and stamping off down the steps of the Four Courts in a raging temper. As the mother went to follow him, our leading barrister grabbed her by the arm to stop her in her tracks and hissed in a voice full of anger, venom and exasperation, 'For God's sake, woman, don't you know your husband's history?' And with that he stomped off in a different direction, leaving the mother standing there dumbfounded.

We didn't have long to wait to find out what he meant, as the next morning Bulldog hit back with renewed diligence and a completely different line of attack. They had dug out the father's history of self-inflicted internment for alcoholism in St Patrick's Hospital. They argued that the man was a confirmed alcoholic with a proven track record. They were able to produce dates and times when he had been in the place. They had details of AA meetings he had attended and suggested that they had available, if required, the head psychiatrist who had treated him, concluding with the argument that, while their gas bottle may have had a minor leak due to some technical malfunction, our case was 'still unproven, Ma Lud'. The father, they maintained, had shown gross negligence in placing the Primus stove in such close proximity to their harmless gas bottle.

'That's absurd, Ma Lud, how do you explain the death of a four-year-old girl lying on the ground some 25 feet away?' retorted our white wig.

But, by the time they had finished, they had presented a case to show that the mere act of lighting the match was nothing short of gross negligence on the part of a certified drunkard. Suddenly, the case had concluded. I didn't quite know what to expect or how it was supposed to end, as my knowledge of court procedure was based on American cases I had seen on TV, in which the defence and then the prosecution got up and gave a final rousing speech demanding justice. In our case Bulldog, after he had seen off their final witness, informed the judge that they had finished. Whereby the old beak asked our lot if they had anything else to offer, resulting in a lot of muttering from our table until, with nods of agreement, one of the wigs jumped up and roared out, 'No Ma Lud.'

With that, the judge pounded his wooden hammer on his desk and declared to all that he would now retire, but that before he passed judgement and awarded any settlement, he wanted to see me privately in his chambers, which nearly caused me to faint with fright.

Within seconds I became the centre of attention. The court clerk beckoned me from my seat and, along with the mother who was to accompany me, we set off through a side door and down a short corridor, before finally being ushered into the judge's chambers. He was seated at his desk, in an open-necked shirt held up with blue braces, as he had removed all of his regalia. Without his 'working clothes' he appeared almost normal. After asking me a few questions regarding Catherine's death, he requested me to show him my scars. I felt like a performer who had made the big time, because now

I was even stripping for a high-court judge. After peering at the scars he compared them to a set of colour photographs he had of my body, taken well over a year before. Then he told me to get dressed, saying that he wanted to have a quick chat with the mother. I left and rejoined the mob that had adjourned to the main hall. The father didn't look impressed with the events that had taken place and especially with the gas company trying to insinuate that he was a drunkard and an alcoholic to boot.

The drive home that evening was silent, with none of the usual banter between the parents regarding the day's happenings. The mother stared straight ahead, emitting a force field of hostility towards the father, which was ten times worse than if she had been roaring and screaming at him. When we got home the father didn't make any attempt to enter the house; he just got out of the car and went straight across the road to the Workman's Club.

The following morning, to a hushed court, the judge made his deliberation. He was awarding us £11,500 in compensation, including costs, which made our barristers and solicitors breathe an audible sigh of relief, as I am sure their bills racked up to over double that amount. After the commotion died down, with the law people jubilant and the parents devastated, there was more to come. He then broke down the numbers to show how he had arrived at this figure. In the eyes of the court, since Catherine was only four, her death was worth £3,000, of which I (being her brother) was to get one third, the parents the rest. Out of the total settlement, my parents were to get a final payment of £8,000. I was also being given £2,500 in consideration of my scars, bringing my total to £3,500. And I was to be made a ward of court until the age of twenty-one.

Not understanding what he was saying, at first I thought

he was going to lock me up for the next eight years; well, a 'ward of court' did sound serious. Later one of our barristers explained that the courts were going to hold the money for me until I reached the age of twenty-one, at which time I would be entitled to collect it, plus the compound interest that it would have gained over the years. Out in the hallway the father had collared the head of our solicitors' firm and was demanding that we appeal the verdict.

'Eleven and a half thousand pounds, with us only getting eight, that will just barely pay our bills. I want you to go back in there and demand an appeal.'

'That is precisely what the Calor Gas company is doing right at this minute, but I don't think they will succeed, as that judge's word is normally final.'

'Three thousand pounds for my daughter – is he completely mad and inhumane?'

'Well, you know the argument the defence has put forward, especially with your past record. It could have been a lot worse: he could have found in favour of the gas company. All in all the compensation figure isn't that bad.'

At that point I thought the father was going to take a swing at him.

'What do you mean? You're all the same, nothing but a bunch of shysters, you lot got together and worked it all out between you, didn't you, how much will all of your bills come to?'

'Given the circumstances, I think that you did all right. You never told us about your drink problem; if you had, we could have been better prepared for the evidence when it was presented.'

'What has my drinking to do with a faulty gas bottle?'

'Prove it, Mr Heaps. Prove it.' And with that last remark, he left the father boiling with temper, standing in the middle of the hallway of the Four Courts.

The father was quite right in his arithmetic: the eight grand would just about cover the cost of the new car and the bills that had accumulated from months of living in hotels and general spending in anticipation of a huge amount of 'compo'.

The new life we had been planning had vanished with the judge's verdict and I watched the destruction of the parents' dreams with mounting concern.

Oh yes, I had had my dreams as well. I, too, had been caught up in the 'promised-land' euphoria, dreaming of a farm in the country with white-railed fences marking its long driveway. With bay horses grazing in green fields, of a different school, in a different area where, perhaps, we could live as a family once more. And, while I never imagined replacing Catherine, I did hope perhaps to have other brothers and sisters.

But I was young and had a very fertile imagination. I could dream my dreams and, if they were not to be realised, then I had a lifetime in front of me to turn new dreams into reality. The parents felt as if they had rolled the dice and lost the throw; they were fated for a life in Emmett Road, with no escape.

If the suggestion of 'compo' had never arisen after the accident, I believe they would have had the courage and strength to endure the sorrow and come through it. Without the hope of free money they could have built again over the ruins of the tragedy that had damaged and reshaped our lives. Now, for the parents in particular, sorrow turned to bitterness. Bitterness with nobody and with everybody, with life in general. We all blamed ourselves; we all blamed each other.

Even as we sat in the high court listening to the Calor Gas barristers presenting their case, we had begun to doubt ourselves. We had begun to wonder if there was some truth in their version of events and now came the time for questions. Questions that brought no satisfactory answers, only more questions.

Maybe the Primus stove did blow up and sever the pipeline connecting the cylinder to the caravan, as they had claimed was possible.

Maybe the father had been on the bottle that day and was completely inebriated.

Why wasn't I missed? Why had nobody come to my assistance to help me put out the flames that were consuming me?

If the mother had reacted more quickly, could she have rushed over and plucked Catherine from the burning mattress before she was mortally injured?

Should the father have reacted faster, too, and also concentrated on saving Catherine?

So many 'ifs'. So many 'maybes'.

So much doubt that, at times, it would push aside any rational thought.

Why did the judge make me a ward of court? Was this normal practice with a juvenile? Or was it that he hadn't trusted the parents to manage my share of the award?

The father blamed himself, because he had lit the match that had set the whole thing off. He had not noticed a leak in the gas bottle that he had bought only a few days before; he had been the one who had brought over the Primus stove; and, in his own mind, it began to seem as if he had caused the accident. He also blamed the mother for not allowing us to play as we had requested. In his grief he turned to an old friend for peace and solitude: his old friend alcohol. Under its influence he would shout out his accusations. He blamed our solicitors for conniving with the opposition. He blamed the Calor Gas company for supplying the bottle in the first place and, especially, he blamed the bastards for getting away with it. But mostly he blamed the mother for not allowing Catherine and me to go off and play.

The mother blamed herself for not allowing us to play. She blamed herself for coming away without any burns or injuries and, because the mother was a trained nurse, she concluded that perhaps she could have done more for Catherine before they brought her to the hospital. It had also been her idea that we go down to Tramore, since I had been out of school with the damaged kneecap. The mother, too, found a new friend: she embraced the father's old one. Under the spell of alcohol the mother blamed the father for giving me the bike against her wishes, which led to me bashing my knee, which led to us going to Tramore when I should have been at school. The mother blamed me for having the forbidden bike and hurting my knee, thus forcing her to make the decision to stop us from playing. She repeated endlessly that if I hadn't hurt my knee none of us would have been in Tramore in the first place. In her drunkenness she would spit out at me that the father had ruined me anyway, and then she would go into a state oscillating between rage and appalling distress. In this condition she would demand, with tears streaming from her eyes and mucous from the nose, why I hadn't been taken in preference to Catherine, instead of being scarred to remind her daily of her loss?

But I alone knew where the full blame lay. I knew who was solely responsible, and it was not the father or the mother. In that split second when I had looked up, I had seen the father's match as it touched the invisible layer of gas and flared out, as if his fingers had gained magical powers of fire, before reaching the Primus stove.

I saw the yellow ball of flame thundering towards me.

I saw the ground burning.

I saw Catherine's mattress explode in yellow flames.

And I was the one who had ridden a bike recklessly through the streets of Dublin. There (according to the law of averages) I should have been, if not killed, at least seriously injured. Instead, for all my bravado, I had only ended up with a badly bruised kneecap, thus writing the script for the final act that resulted in Catherine's death.

I had been left to live on, so that every time I took off my shirt and viewed myself in a mirror, the scars would act as a reminder of my folly. I took refuge in my own company and spent hours in my room. There a new thought began to develop: maybe there was a reason why I had been left to live, perhaps the gods had not quite finished with me yet?

Catherine's clothes had been left in exactly the same place as on the day we had departed for Tramore. Her photographs were enlarged and placed all around the house. Catherine's grave became a shrine that every visitor to the house was brought to see.

At the time I could not understand why this was happening. If I had, I might have found it easier to comprehend the events of the next few years, while the parents began to try for more children. Every time that hope flickered to life, the father would go around the house singing, 'Googy back again, Googy back again', 'Googy' being the pet name that he had called Catherine. Then there would come the disappointment when the mother miscarried yet again.

He even told me that he had written a song in Catherine's memory, which he had me learn off by heart: 'You are my sunshine, my only sunshine, you make me happy when skies are grey, you'll never know dear, how much we love you, so come back . . .' One day I turned on the radio and heard it being played and when I asked him about it he said that he had had it published in her memory. More lies. By now he was getting to the stage at which he was incapable of telling the truth.

The father then suggested to the mother that he could have a child by another woman. It appeared that the mother could not now go the full nine months and, because the child of another woman would be half his, we could bring it up as our own and get Catherine back that way. Adoption was also looked at, but I think they never made it past the first round with the adoption board.

'Well, look what you did with the last bunch of kids you had in your care; you went and got them all blown up. Now you want us to give you some more? I don't think so.'

In this new home environment I learned to survive in the best way that I could. Over the next few years the mother began to accuse me of thinking only of myself, with no regard for anybody else. Perhaps she was right and I could have been a better son for her, been there for her. But I didn't, and I wasn't.

Cupid Strikes

IT WAS A beautiful summer's morning in June. I had just finished another year in school and, more importantly, completed my intermediate exams. It was the summer of 1970. Hippy power was in, with their 'make peace not war' philosophy ruling the streets of Dublin, especially around the Stephen's Green area. I was fifteen years old, heading down to Boulta for the summer holidays, and was once again taking the train out of Kingsbridge Station. I was quite pleased with the way my exams had gone, but I would have to wait until late summer before the official results came out. I knew that I had blown Irish, but that didn't bother me too much as I had completely written the subject off as a bad job anyway. I was resigning myself to the fact that, in my case, seeing inside the grounds of a university was an unlikely event.

The train pulled out of the station and began its now familiar journey south. I was heading for freedom from Emmett Road, going to spend another few months on Matty's farm where I could forget the rowing parents and the screaming fights, which had escalated into bitter conflicts typified by accusations and, at times, undisguised hatred. By this time the mother, when drunk, had taken to accusing the father of destroying their case and would work herself into such a frenzy that he had to call a doctor from the dispensary and have her sedated.

A party was to be held at Boulta that evening and my cousin Pat had ensured that I received an invitation, as all of my uncles, aunts and cousins were to be present. But the reason that my pulse was beating faster and I was experiencing a feeling of anticipation, fear and apprehension all rolled into one, was that Gina was also invited. Over the two years since that first, fateful night at the pictures, I had often seen her during my excursions down to the farm. Mostly on a Sunday morning, when she and her older sister, Marigold, called into the farmyard to collect one or both of my cousins for a day's hunting. On those occasions she would be on her pony, looking confident, straight-backed and totally at ease. It was as if all of the other sounds in the yard faded out when I saw her perched up there, her smile lighting up her face like the sun breaking through black clouds on an overcast winter's day. I could only hear my heart beating violently against ribs that I thought could not restrain its pounding. I would already have spent the morning rehearsing what I thought were witty and amusing lines, in an attempt to win her over with my outstanding dialogue. But as soon as her eyes settled on my face I always turned into a complete, babbling buffoon. My vocal cords would seize up and emit only grunting noises that surprised even me, while at the same time my face turned the colour of a ripe tomato.

And so here I was, sitting in a half-empty train carriage, trying to restrain my apprehension and hoping that when I set eyes on Gina again I would not revert to a stammering Dublin idiot. Accepting that worrying over something that might not happen was not going to solve the problem, I settled down and let the train's rhythmic noises lull me into a semi-conscious reverie.

In this state, my drifting thoughts alternated between

rehearsing that night's opener to Gina ('Hi, Gina, my name is Eeeeee, Ee, Ee . . .') and skimming forward to the future. I wanted to become an engineer. I wanted to build bridges, dams and aeroplanes. I wanted to start with a large, clean sheet of paper and draw out some of my inner visions – and to gain the qualifications necessary to transform those dream designs into reality. To be a part of creating something new that might remind generations to come of my existence on this planet. I had spent hours studying the qualifications I would need to join University College Dublin, just around the corner from my school in Leeson Street. I could see that I would have to concentrate on maths and art over the next two years – both subjects I was good at. But of course there was also the Irish – at which I was useless. But, being the optimist, I still hoped for the miracle needed to get a D (at least) in my Irish Leaving Cert. exam paper.

'Hello Gina, great to see . . . see . . . se . . . se . . .' No, same problem. Even when I talked to her in my head I stuttered as if I were sending a message in Morse code. What was it about this person that I couldn't string two words together from the comfort and safety of my train carriage? Think about something else. Over the past few years, since the court case, the parents had been behaving like fiddlers' elbows: as soon as one of them came out of hospital, the other would check in. In the father's case, he had dispensed with St Pats. I suspect that they took his drying-out periods too seriously and attempted to cure him with a week of 'cold turkey', before plugging him into the nearest socket for the electric shock treatment. No, he had found a much better place called St John of Gods, which not only had the same indoor facilities as St Pats, but also boasted a nine-hole golf course. Here was the equivalent of a five-star hotel, and all being paid for by the health insurance company.

Whenever the mother was in hospital he would suggest that we 'visit the mother, and then go on to the hotel in Bray for a drink'. However, the hotel seemed to attract lots of lovely young ladies, to whom the father had taken a fancy. We reached the stage at which I had to call him 'Ron' in public, instead of 'Dad', if he was forced to take me with him. Better still (from his point of view, since I kept on forgetting myself), he'd say, 'Here's a few bob, go off and spend it somewhere else.'

I have no idea of what kind of success he enjoyed with the young ladies, especially with me loitering in the background, but we made many visits to the mother during that period. Of course it was harder to get rid of a lad of fifteen, so maybe that's what prompted him to contact the navy in England and request that I take the entrance exam to see if I could become a cadet with Her Majesty's finest. I would have been accepted, but for failing the medical on the grounds that I was as blind as a bat.

'Hi Gina, good to see you again. How are the horses going?' Yes, that was much better.

I hadn't noticed that the train had pulled into Cork station. Rousing myself from my daydream, I walked the short distance to the bus stop to catch the bus to Midleton, where Pat was to collect me. It was only a twenty-minute trip and, while I hung around waiting for Pat's arrival, I noticed a girl nearby who was also loitering with intent. When Pat arrived and called out a greeting to both of us, I realised that she, too, was joining the evening's festivities. Unfortunately, as I played the gentleman and placed our luggage in the boot of the car, Pat roared out across the car roof, 'You'll be happy to know that Gina is going to be there tonight.'

My face turned bright red (a colour I was quickly beginning to associate with that name) and my speech impediment rushed back at the very thought of meeting her. Perhaps I would just let Pat make the formal introductions while I hovered close by, trying not to look like a complete berk who had just been let out of the asylum on parole.

Pat and her friend Ruth chatted on the drive to the farm, while I relaxed in the back seat and drifted off into my inner world once more.

Our shop was closed again. For how long it would be closed on this occasion, I had no idea. It appeared to be operating without any rhyme or reason. Whenever the parents did reopen it, they ran it with none of their former zeal, keeping it poorly stocked, with shabbily dressed display windows. Last year the father had reopened and hired a shop assistant to run it while the mother was in hospital. Actually 'assistants' would be more correct: they only ever lasted a week or two at best, although at first I couldn't fathom the reason for their brief tenure. Then I realised that he was coming home during the day and attempting to expand their job descriptions so that they were responsible not only for looking after the shop's needs, but his own as well.

But it was a more recent 'incident' that absorbed me as we travelled from Midleton out to the farm. I had arrived home unexpectedly early from school one evening and, finding the shop closed again, had let myself in through the hall door. While passing the father's room, I'd heard him in bed with his secretary from the office. I'd made myself scarce, since I didn't want him to know that I had 'caught him in the act', but I was still wrestling with the problem of whether or not to tell the mother when the car arrived at Boulta.

The house was in uproar, with people rushing around everywhere cheerfully attempting to make ready for the party, which was scheduled to start in an hour. The house had, in effect, been divided into two separate sections. The parlour and front dining-room were to be given over to Matty's brothers, sisters, and special guests. The kitchen area was to be left to the 'children', who numbered around thirty when all of the cousins had been tallied. One of my distant relations had been placed in charge of our group; he was a few years older than the rest of us and nicknamed the Kipper, for reasons totally unknown to me. Matty had given him explicit instructions not to let any of us have alcohol, except for the mild punch that his wife and Pat had prepared. I found the Kipper in the front kitchen setting up the record-player, since he had also elected himself DJ for the evening. He was a large fellow who sported a constantly lopsided grin that suggested mischievous acts in the making. When I called out a greeting to him, he nodded 'hello' and beckoned me to follow as he headed for the back door. For some reason or another, I could never understand one word that he spoke; to make matters worse, he had a habit of speaking out of the side of his mouth without opening his lips.

As soon as we hit the safety of the backyard, beyond range of prying eyes, he produced a full whiskey bottle and, taking a swig, handed it over to me for sampling. So much for Matty's choice of custodian.

'Grrruaght to seeee wyoour, heeeps, whayooou doooing?'

Hoping that he had just said that it was great to see me, I responded with a similar comment. Then, lowering his voice, he continued, 'Cehween thee gireels finnnish crewith thee pounche, I cwarant wyoou to poooor the concotenncees of theeeis innntooo the booollleee, goootiiitt heeeeps? Iaaave alssso gotttenn a feeeeww mmoore in theee bacck off the caaar.'

I pieced together what he was after since, thankfully, he used hand gestures as well. He wanted me to put the contents of that whiskey bottle and the others he had stored in the back of his car into the punch-bowl when nobody was looking. Taking another swig from his proffered bottle, I told him not to worry and departed as quickly as I could to avoid any further conversation with him, no matter how short.

At just after seven o'clock my aunts and uncles began to arrive with their children in tow. Some opted to come in the front way and had no need of a bell to announce them, as the door had a habit of sticking: the noise of bodies banging and crashing against the front door while they attempted to gain entry was more than ample to herald their arrival. The smart ones, not having brought their battering-rams with them, opted for the back entrance. Here, with kisses for our aunts and handshakes for our uncles, they passed on through the kitchen into the parlour, leaving their offspring to swell our number. This method seemed to involve a good fifteen minutes for the obligatory greetings.

Our grandfather Pappy (or 'the Godfather', as he was referred to by all) arrived early, dressed in his dark, three-piece suit, complete with bowler hat. He spent the evening sitting on a straight-backed chair in the centre of the room, presiding over the festivities. Nearly blind from being kicked in the head by a horse at the age of ninety, he was still a large and powerful man, sound of body and limb; he smoked his pipe and drank glasses of whiskey as if it was water. When he required a refill, he would hold up his empty glass and shout out, 'Blazes, is there no drink to be got in this household? Bring me my belongings and take me to a proper pub.'

Our uncle Joe, after a few glasses of whiskey, got up and danced on the living-room table, while scattering plates and cutlery in every direction and totally ignoring his wife's pleas to 'come down you fool, before you end up breaking your other leg'. Joe had broken his leg while on honeymoon, riding one of his horses in a race, and was constantly reminded of this event by the rest of his family.

Hanna (another sister) and her husband, Dan, arrived along with their three children. They were kindly people who didn't get involved with the family rows, as they were too busy trying to carve out an existence on the patch of mountain they called their farm. Dan's only concern throughout the course of any social gathering would be to assess the time when he could go out to his car and bring in his fiddle, which he brought along for all special occasions. It sounded like a catfight breaking out when he put bow to string and always caused an instant outcry from the rest of the family. Inevitably, as this particular evening wore on and the effects of copious quantities of whiskey took over, he eventually unleashed it from its resting-place and began to play, drawing the usual response from one of his brothers-in-law.

'Agh, Jesus, Matty, who told him he could bring it in? Sure, Christ, it sounds like he's sawing timber.' Matty, ignoring the comment, jumped onto the piano stool in the parlour, and began to beat out a melody to accompany the woodcutting.

Auntie Ruby turned up with her son and daughter. It was hard to believe that Ruby was part of the same large family, as she was totally different to the rest of them. She was small-framed, but more than compensated for her diminutive stature when she got drunk – and it usually only took about two glasses of whiskey to get the ball rolling. We monitored her progress from a distance and drew lots to see which one of us would go over and wind her up with her favourite topic. When the time was deemed right, especially since she was sitting down by herself, the lucky winner embarked on the following conversation.

'Evening, Auntie Ruby, how are you tonight, enjoying the party?'

'Ha, ha, augh, sure, grand, grand altogether, ha, ha.'

'A few of us were just talking about farmers and especially about farmers not having to pay taxes. We believe that's not right and they should be taxed like the rest of the working population, Auntie Ruby, what do you think?'

'What? What? What did you say?' And her eyes instantly became bloodshot with the explosion of some vessel at the rapid rise in blood pressure.

'I said, I thought that all farmers should pay taxes.'

'That's what I thought you said you basstaard. You hear me, you're nothing but a bassstared. All before you were bassstarrreds, you rotten basstarred.'

With that she jumped up. (At times, owing to her height, it was hard to tell if she was standing or not.) Gripping the table with both hands she upended it, screaming, 'Your father was a basstarred before you, you're nothing but a rotten basstarrded, you bastard.' At that point whoever had pulled the short straw slunk away, leaving her to her rant until one of her children rushed over to settle her down, wildly searching around the room for the culprit who had started her off.

After the customary greeting ritual had been completed, we slipped away into our own area and surrounded the punch-bowl, which I had fortified with the contents of the Kipper's car boot. It tasted foul, but after a few glasses it numbed the mouth into acceptance. While I was wondering what would happen if I spilt some on the concrete floor (figuring that it might just eat through the concrete), Gina arrived with her sister Marigold. I didn't have to see or be told of her arrival, I felt it in the form of a shock wave that hit me like a sledgehammer. And, sure enough, when I turned around I saw her smiling and nodding at friends as she entered the lower kitchen (they must have opted to come in via the front door).

Since the Kipper had set himself up as DJ for the evening, he decided that he was going to run a 'Top Ten' as one of the

evening's highlights and announced to the room in general
that the dancing was about to commence. Well, I can't say that
this was what he actually said, because it was so noisy that he
could have been telling everybody the place was on fire. But
since the music came on and everybody got up to dance, I can
only assume that he must have said something along those
lines.

Gina looked radiant, dressed in white jeans and an off-
white, fluffy woollen jumper. Casting all thoughts of
introduction aside, I simply walked up to her and asked her if
she wanted to dance. And that was that, we danced the night
away to the sounds of the Kipper's Top Ten, with constant
replays – especially of the current number one, 'Whiskey in
the Jar'. Around midnight I asked Gina if she would like to
take a walk with me and she nodded her agreement. We
slipped out the back door leaving the gang pounding the floor
to another chorus of 'with me ring, for a do, for a da; [stamp,
stamp, stamp, stamp] rock for me da-di-oh, there's whiskey in
the jar'. We headed down the tree-lined driveway with no
specific destination in mind. Mesmerised by her presence at
my side, it seemed to me that our feet were our navigators as
we gazed up at the night's glory.

A full moon had risen in a cloudless sky, bathing the road
in front of us with a soft, golden splendour of dancing
shadows. Before long we arrived at a lovely stone bridge that
spanned a brook, and the sound of water hurrying over the
stones, as if on a mission, echoed up to us through its arches.
Peering over the wall, we gazed in wonder, for the moonlight
had transformed the dark waters of the brook into a riot of
sparkling silver droplets as its waters filtered and bounced over
large pebbles. We turned together, as if on cue, and our heads
touched. From there it was the most natural thing in the world
to slowly lean down and search out her lips with mine. That

first kiss dissolved all the uncertainties I had felt until that moment. I finally understood the feeling that I had carried around inside me those past two years, from the very first moment I had set eyes on her. I knew with an adult's certainty that I was totally in love with this creature who had transformed me from a competent being into a babbling moron. Eventually, arm in arm, as if we had known each other for decades, we made our way slowly back to the party, planning our next meeting. Confident that, in spite of our youth, we were the only people in the world for each other.

On our return we found the place in turmoil, as if a murder had been committed in our absence – or, worse still, as if somebody had upset Auntie Ruby again. However, as soon as Matty set eyes on me, I quickly realised that I had generated the hullabaloo. Gina and I had been missed and apparently, although we had taken no notice of the time, we had been away for hours. Gina was whisked home and I was told that I would be sent packing the next morning on the first available bus to Dublin. Thankfully Matty relented the following day and, as we had really done nothing wrong, he was unable to chastise me over the incident. Throughout the remainder of my stay there (which was cut short, because my parents came down to collect me) Gina and I stole as much time together as we possibly could.

We came alive in each other's company. We laughed and joked about the silliest things and we bantered that 'anything she could do, I could do better'. (This last was to become the constant postscript in our letters to each other.) We held hands and dreamt about a future that we would make together, we built rockets in our hearts and flew them to the stars. We passed the summer weeks like caterpillars that had metamorphosed into wonderfully colourful butterflies, knowing that they had only a short time to live and wanting to experience every moment fully. I returned to Dublin with promises that we would write to each other. Sitting in the back of the car listening to my parents squabbling, I felt that my heart was going to break, because every revolution of the car's wheels was taking me further and further away from her. Nothing could raise my spirits.

When we arrived back in Dublin, the mother informed me that she was going to go back nursing in St James's Hospital. The shop was to be put up for sale and the father was going to check himself into St John of Gods – and this time he was determined to dry out.

I was totally in love with the most beautiful creature that I had ever set eyes on. She was in County Cork and I was in Dublin with a totally uncertain future. I searched for the strength to continue living in an environment that was plagued day and night with rows and accusations. With the feeling that I had left a greater part of me behind with Gina, a depression set in that threatened to overpower me. The parents were now threatening to sell the only thing that gave me any sense of security. I thought seriously about leaving home and taking to the streets. And then I contemplated contacting Matty, enlisting Pat's help, and requesting that I work on his farm.

I dismissed that idea as soon as I thought it. It might bring me temporarily closer to Gina but, in the long run, I would end up as a farm hand. I realised that one day, if I made that choice, I would have to watch as Gina set up home with somebody else (somebody who could offer her a lot more than a dreary farm helper's cottage in the wilderness) and I knew that would wrench my heart out. Even worse, she might fall in love with one of my cousins and end up living in Boulta. My mind ran wild with crazy thoughts, and that did not improve my mental stability one little bit. I was determined that no matter how long it took, wherever I ended up having to travel, whatever hardships I went through, some day the two of us would eventually be together.

For the remainder of that week I begged, pleaded and cajoled the mother into changing her mind. I suggested that I could now leave school and run the shop full-time, which was flatly refused. Both parents were adamant: for better or worse, I was to continue with my schooling. With four weeks left before I returned to start my fifth year, we reached a compromise. We would keep my home (at least for the present), and I could reopen the shop, restock and re-establish the business, while the father dried out for the 'last time'. The mother would return to nursing when the father came out. We would also hire a competent person to run the shop after I went back to school. The next day I set out with tremendous energy to clean up the shop, burning all the rubbish, sweeping, and cleaning the windows. There was quite a bit of stock still gathering dust on the shelves, so the next item on my agenda was to take stock and work out my next orders.

The father had taken the car into St John of God's with him, because the mother couldn't drive. I spent a whole week visiting wholesalers and lugging the stuff back home on the 21A bus, which caused me a great deal of trouble. The really heavy items, such as the dartboards from Millard Brothers, I strapped on the back of my bike. But, after the first attempt, the weight of the load blew out the back tyre, so I resorted to taking them, one at a time, on the bus. I was open for business within a week and David called in every day to give me a hand.

More importantly, Gina's first letter arrived. On opening it, I immediately jumped to the last line – when I read the words 'all of my love' at the bottom, I was able to return to the beginning and read the whole without mounting apprehension. That same evening I sat down and attempted to respond, scribbling words in block letters, which were spelt so badly that I worried I would never again hear from her. But all through the remainder of that summer, her letters kept coming with the now familiar 'all of my love' signature.

Very quickly I was back in school, the shop was kept open with a new assistant, the father was back home from drying out, and the mother had returned to nursing.

During Christmas week our shop assistant quit because she wanted to join her brother in England. At least that was what she told us, but a few days later I spotted her walking down O'Connell Street, so perhaps she quit for another reason. The mother had opted to work Christmas Eve and Day at the hospital, with the plan being that the father and I joined her in the hospital canteen for Christmas lunch. This left David and I working on our own in the shop on Christmas Eve. Gone were the days when the shop was black with people and we had to have lots of serving staff.

That Christmas Eve the shop barely ticked over to the sound of the occasional customer nipping in for a last-minute present; times had changed, and most people now bought their presents well in advance of the so-called Christmas rush. No more would 'Everybody's' on Emmett Road reverberate to Boy-o-Boy's voice as he passed out drink to eager hands selling toys to punters caught up in the fever pitch of buying their Christmas presents. The father spent the day commuting back and forth from the shop to the Workman's Club, and David went home around eight, disappointed that the rush of shoppers he recalled from Christmases past had never materialised. I stood behind the counter until the last person had left the street, hoping, forever hoping, that the bright lights of the shop windows exploding out onto the pavement of the otherwise darkened street would draw a last minute press.

Around midnight I finally gave up and closed the shop

doors. I didn't know it, but I was doing it for the last time. I had taken in exactly £140 that day. When the father returned from the pub, completely paralytic, he refused to believe my tally and accused me of having pocketed the large outstanding balance that he was expecting. This resulted in us having a stand-up row and, when I finally retreated to my room, I wished that I were back down on Matty's farm, where I was sure they were preparing for a Christmas Day without the arguments. I also thought of Gina, no doubt riding in the St Stephen's Day hunt; at that point in time I absolutely regretted ever having been introduced into Matty's family.

I felt as if I was playing a role in *Through the Looking Glass*. Mine was an upside-down, chaotic world but I had been given a brief vision of what family life could be, a life that I would never have, or be part of. I paced my room, which because of its size was always cold, not looking forward to lunch in the hospital, but realising that at least it had its plus side. The mother couldn't drink while on duty, so that was a promise of one argument less. My mind drifted back to Gina. I read all of her letters once more and decided that, come the New Year, I would have to rethink my strategy for breaking out of this environment I was living in. And, most importantly, when was I going to see her again?

I was sixteen years old and had decided that I needed three items in my life. Money was the first, which would lead to the second, a motor bike, which would then put me in contact with the third, Gina. How I was missing her, but her letters still arrived, giving me a wonderful insight into what was happening down in County Cork; and they were still signed with 'all of my love'. At times her stories of recent events included the names of people I wasn't familiar with and sparked chords of jealousy within me, because these faceless people were spending time with her, while I was so far away.

Why did I think that life was unfair?

Having come up with a relatively simple plan, all I had to do was acquire the first item on my list and the rest would fall into place. To get some money, I had to get a job in the evenings. Moreover, a job that the mother would not find out about, which might be a bit tricky, since she had issued a mandate stating that I was to study at home during the school terms for the next two years to ensure that I passed my Leaving Cert.

However, I had other ideas, ideas that didn't involve me being incarcerated in my room for five hours every evening. Anyway, now that we were fifth formers, the school was treating us a bit more like adults, with the result that we had plenty of study time during the day. It was on the way home from school one evening that I had my first idea for raising the cash needed to get the bike of my dreams. South Circular Road was described as 'flat land'. Lying close to St James's Hospital, most of the houses there had been converted into bedsits and were occupied by country folk, whose only communication with their loved ones back home was by letter or telephone.

I was passing a local phone box on one particular evening when I noticed a lad hammering the daylights out of the pay machine in an attempt to get his money back, as it had obviously jammed before he could make his call. The next day I decided to experiment with one of the phone boxes just outside the rear entrance to the hospital, by the Rialto gates. My plan was relatively simple: using a pencil, a piece of fine thread and a nice bit of soft cardboard, I jammed the lump of cardboard as far up the refund slot as it would go, out of reach of curious fingers, assuming that the thin thread attached to it would pass unnoticed. The idea was that a person would put money into the slot to make their call and press button A, but if no one was home on the other end of the line, he or she would give up and press button B. No money would be refunded because my cardboard would have snagged the change halfway down the refund chute. After a while the person would give up and go away, blaming the phone company for its faulty box. I would return the following day, pull on the string, and pocket the take. It worked so well that I thought about franchising the idea, but then who could I trust? So I mapped out an area for myself, which was on my route home from school, and by the end of the week I was working up to ten phone boxes stuffed with cardboard. This little business was very lucrative while it lasted, but good ideas of this type have a time limit, because something or somebody always comes along and screws them up. In my case, I don't know if somebody reported a fault to the phone company and it discovered my little ploy, or if another person decided that they wanted to get into my business, but the end result was the same. One evening, doing my rounds, I found that all my bits of cardboard had been removed. Not wanting to push my luck, I didn't bother trying to replace them in case the boxes were being watched, and I decided to let that particular idea cool for a while.

My mother always opened my mail with the excuse that since I was living under her roof she had a right to do so. Usually it was only birthday or Christmas cards that she opened and, until my communications with Gina had begun, I really hadn't had any problem with this. Now things were a little different. Unless I caught the postman in the mornings, I would find Gina's letters already opened on the mantelpiece. The other really annoying habit she had was searching my room, going through all of my clothing, sniffing and checking the pockets. She also began my sex education, as she was back nursing full-time. But instead of telling me about 'the birds and the bees' (in which, by then, I was already well versed), she decided to indoctrinate me with the horrors of sexual diseases and the things I would likely catch if I 'did it with loose women'.

During an enforced visit to her ward in St James's Hospital 3 she pointed out the poor unfortunates dying of syphilis, hopping around the place with their brains fried up. What she achieved was to put me off sex for years, because I now believed I would end up catching something fatal. The only advice my father ever gave me on the subject was 'Son, always stay away from fast women, as you normally can't catch them; stick to the slow ones!'

For about a month I had been canvassing the owner of the Jet petrol station at Kilmainham Cross to give me a part-time job and at last he had an opening on the evening and weekend shifts. I started on the six o'clock to midnight shift at a pound a night, two pounds on Saturdays, and three on Sundays. Most of the people who called in were only looking for ten bob's worth of petrol – and expected me to carry out what amounted to a complete service of their car on top of that. This was especially frustrating on wet nights when they drove up to the pumps. There I would be, soaking wet because the garage had no canopy worth talking about, while they wound down their car windows about an inch, allowing a blast of hot air to escape and brush against my freezing face.

'Jaysus you look wet, wha'? Here, shove ten bob into her, check the oil, water and tyres. Jaysus, it's bleeden' freezing out there,' and up would go the window.

Realising that, on my wages, I would be waiting a long time for my bike (which the owner was holding for me), I decided I needed to supplement my income a little bit. So on the wet and windy nights I began to get into the swing of things.

'Sorry Mister, the air pump isn't working for the tyres, but she took two pints of oil; that will be another ten bob.' I would close his bonnet and throw the empty oil containers into the rubbish bin right in front of him.

'Jaysus wha'? Two bleeden' pints? Fecking hell, she never burned a drop before.'

'Look Mister, you asked me to check the oil. I told you, I put two pints into her, do you want to see the containers I've thrown away?'

Grumbling, he would hand over another ten bob note as if it was my fault that his car burned so much oil – and, actually, it was. For as soon as he drove away, I would retrieve the two full bottles of oil from the bin and return them to the stand, having added another ten shillings to my motor-bike fund.

Easter arrived and I was heading down to the farm again. When Gina and I met up again after all those months, it was as if we had just said goodbye the previous evening; the months washed away as if they had never existed. She took the opportunity to comment on my spelling and, amazingly, it seemed that she always understood exactly what I wrote. Apparently she had no worries in leaving any of my letters lying around, because nobody else had a hope of deciphering them. Every evening we met up and talked about everything under the sun – except about my home in Dublin. Perhaps her intuition told her that I did not want to talk about my parents, or perhaps she felt that I would speak about them when the time was right.

All too soon the holiday came to an end and I was on my way back home. By the time the train pulled into Kingsbridge Station, I had already scribed a note to Gina and my first task on alighting was to go in search of a post box. Having blown all of my motor-bike money on socialising during the holidays, it was back to the evening work in the petrol station. Once again I was faced with the dilemma of how to raise the money in the shortest possible time without ending up in Artane Correctional Centre. Puncture repair was one way to increase my nightly wage, since the owner let me keep half of the rate if I did the repairs after six or on the weekends. Charging a pound a time to fix the odd puncture in the evenings certainly helped; however, there weren't enough cars getting flat tyres to make much difference to my fund, especially when I had to serve petrol at the same time. But the fellow who had hired me had never suggested that I couldn't subcontract the work.

Enter David. The plan was that I would share my portion of the puncture repair with him as long as he tended the cars. There was one slight problem: we now needed to increase the volume of repairs to make it worth our while. Lavan's hardware shop supplied the solution to that dilemma in the form of a couple of boxes of carpet tacks. Each evening we would 'accidentally' drop a handful of tacks at various intersections in our immediate area. It worked marvellously, sales soared tenfold. The scheme had something in common with modern marketing campaigns, in that we were selling our customers something they hadn't realised they needed until ten minutes before they met us. And our service was impressive: we were always able to identify the cause of the puncture immediately and rectify it at speed. More importantly, we regained our tacks for recycling. Like many good ideas, we went overboard one weekend and achieved an all-time record of thirty-six repairs, which made the garage owner not only raise his eyebrows, but also accuse me outright of having a personal hand in these misfortunes. We had to curtail our operation somewhat after that, but I was over halfway towards getting my bike. Only one more good idea and I would have it within a few weeks – and that is what I told the owner of the bike.

It was quite by accident that the next brainwave hit me

one evening as I was serving a customer who had called in with his usual 'Hey sonny, fill her up or put a pound into her, whatever comes first.' On opening the flap of his tank I noticed that his petrol cap was missing, which I pointed out to the driver, offering to see if one from our collection of spares would fit his car. Sure enough, I was able to oblige him, which delighted him so much that he gave me ten shillings for my thoughtfulness. It was like a light bulb going off in my head.

Most evenings I locked up at midnight and walked home. From then on I varied my route home in order to temporarily 'borrow' petrol caps from the parked cars lining the empty streets. By the end of the week I had quite a collection in a nice big bag that I kept close by me at all times. Now all I had to do was wait for the owners to turn up for fuel and I would sell them back their petrol caps. The trick was never to give them back their own cap (many of them were painted the same colour as the car); instead, I would give them something similar, which kept them happy.

This little enterprise went so well that within a month I had £47 and was looking forward to collecting my machine on the weekend. I quit my cap borrowing on the day that a local garda dropped into the Jet station, requesting that I contact them immediately regarding an unscrupulous person (or persons) who may have tried to sell me petrol caps. During the past few weeks it had been brought to their attention that petty theft of these caps in our area was on the upturn. As soon as he left, I dumped my growing collection of caps into the nearest litterbin, thinking that I'd better relinquish that particular activity while I was ahead.

David came with me to collect the machine, which I bought for £38 pounds. She was a mighty machine: twin cylinders, four-stroke and went like the clappers. On our way home that Saturday I scared the living daylights out of myself, not to mention David, who was hanging onto the back for dear life. We returned to the Jet station, because I was going to store the bike there until I decided how to break the news of my new acquisition to the mother. David, when he got off, swore that it was the first and last time he would ever get on the back of a bike with me. And, true to his word, no matter how much I tried to convince him that it was dead safe, he never rode with me again – pointing out that it was the word 'dead' that concerned him.

One evening the mother called into the station and caught me serving petrol. I thought she was going to blow a fuse right there on the spot. But, much to my amazement, she just looked at me, turned on her heels and walked away, saying that she would talk to me later when I got home. This was nearly worse than if she had lambasted me there on the spot, as I had to go through the rest of the shift holding imaginary conversations with her and pondering the outcome of this pending confrontation. By the time I got home I was so worked up that I was quite ready to tell her where she could stick her parenthood, the constant rows with the father, her orders, decrees – and anything else I could think of.

The mother must have sensed my potentially defiant attitude, because her reaction was not what I had expected. For the first time in years we sat down in the early hours of the morning, drinking tea and discussing my existence in general. When I told her why I was working in the garage and about the bike, her only comment was that I shouldn't kill myself and that, as the shop was now permanently closed, I could park it in there. We talked of school and many other topics that late-night chats tend to bring out in people. I felt it was the first time in my life that I had been able to sit down with either of my parents and discuss myself, adult to potential adult.

It was a coming of age for the mother as well. I think she

finally realised that I wasn't a two-year-old any more; in fact I was a very streetwise sixteen-year-old who had spent most of the last six years practically fending for himself. During the periods when my mother had been in hospital or away, the father had virtually moved into the Workman's Club and I had had to do all my own cooking and washing. Never ironing. I drew the line there, which meant that I spent most of my time going to school looking as if I had slept in my clothes. When the father was in hospital drying out, the mother always went the other way completely, attempting to impose a highly disciplined regime, which I balked against. It's amazing how three people can view the same subject and come up with three entirely different scenarios. The father saw me, at times, as a hindrance to his own activities, especially when it came to the drink and womanising. The mother (during the times she was embracing motherhood) saw me as an unruly child who required a lot of harsh discipline because, as she put it, 'the father has that child ruined'. I saw myself as the person trapped in the middle, attempting to survive in an environment that I found, at best, difficult. And we all three believed we were correct.

Our conversation that evening cleared the air somewhat, but afterwards I was not able to feel that we had reached an understanding. The mother was now craving for the three of us to begin to act as a family unit, but, as far as I was concerned, too much water had passed under the bridge of life. I was just biding my time until I could move out and try to build a life of my own. As a matter of fact I couldn't wait for the opportunity to bolt, for I refused to believe for one second that a magic wand could be waved over us and that we could all live 'happily ever after'. No sir, that only happened in books and films and I considered myself firmly entrenched in the real world, not fantasy land.

Heaps of Trouble

WHENEVER I WAS with Gina she made me believe it was just fine to be my own true self, with my own capabilities and in charge of my own destiny. She never once made me feel that, in her eyes, I was less than anybody else. I believe that she enjoyed my freethinking spirit, especially my ability to tell people exactly what I thought, which some others found intolerable. On our very first night by that lovely old bridge I think she had seen the 'real' me. She saw through the exterior of bravado, the easy-going and devil-may-care attitude that I portrayed to the world in general; she saw the lost soul inside me craving understanding.

In her I saw exactly the same things. She was also an 'orphan' in her own house, hoping for understanding from family who were too caught up with their own lives. Looking into her eyes as our hearts bonded, I felt that I had finally found the one person that I could really be happy with. Oh, sure, we had some small hurdles to canter over. Nothing that winning the Irish Prize Bonds couldn't sort out; and, since I was forever the optimist, well . . .

∞

I was seventeen years of age and I had finally done it. I had done my Leaving Certificate and, for the last time, I walked out of the school as if I were a prisoner released from a lengthy jail sentence without any parole conditions. Until the results came out I was able to enter the transitional period that only happens once in a person's lifetime. I became a working student, engaged in what would be considered a dead-end job at any other point in my life. I became a porter in St James's Hospital. Here the mother was proudly able to say, 'That's my son, he's only working here for the summer, he's waiting for the results of his Leaving Cert. before he decides what he wants to study at university.' All very acceptable and commendable from the mother's point of view, especially when you are swapping stories with fellow nurses who are explaining to you that their sons and daughters opted to stay at home in bed until they got their results.

'It's the way I brought him up, you know.'

'Well, he's a credit to you. Hasn't he turned out to be a fine young man? You must be very proud of him.'

'It wasn't easy, you know. I had tragedy and . . .'

I grew sick to death of listening to it, but it had been the parents' influence that got me the job, just like the other sons and daughters of Eastern Health Board executives who flooded the place. My role during those summer months was to take over the duties of any porter who was away on his two-week annual holiday, to become a sort of 'stand-in porter-at-large'. The hours were long, but I was paid exactly the same amount as the full-timers were.

I couldn't believe my first pay cheque. I brought it back to the payroll office, thinking that they had made a mistake. Twenty-seven pounds fifty, it was almost as much as the nurses and doctors made; I was rich beyond belief. Of course I didn't tell the mother, as she would have wanted most of it.

I had learned that lesson the hard way the previous summer, when working for Monty, the old Jew in the cash and carry, who paid me five and a half quid a week for a twelve-hour day. The mother took the fiver and left me with the rest, consoling me with the words, 'You may think this is hard, but that is what a son's role in life is all about; you have to look after your mother.' Then she dashed off across the street to show the neighbours what her son had handed over to her from his first week's wage packet.

The parents were in particularly good form one evening when I returned from the hospital. I was informed that they had sold our shop for 'a hell of an amount of money' to the Eastern Health Board. Apparently the Board wanted to move the dispensary from its present location on the fringes of the old Keogh Square, because it was broken into so often these days that they might just as well not bother locking up in the evenings. Even though the Health Board didn't want to take possession of our building for about eight months, they were going to pay the parents the full amount as soon as the solicitors could conclude the transaction. So the parents could vacate the building and move into their new home on a modern housing estate that had just been built in the Malahide area of North Dublin.

I had taken no interest whatsoever in any of these proceedings, since they had been discussing this for over a year. My attitude was that I'd believe it when I saw it, for I had become hardened to hearing about so many plans that came to naught. Anyway, I wasn't thinking that far ahead, as my immediate concern was my latest placement at the hospital, which started the following Monday morning. Monday rolled around and at 7 a.m., still half asleep, I dragged myself into my new territory: for the next fortnight I was going to be the hospital's 'spuds apprentice'.

I gazed with mounting concern at the equipment that produced the mountain of potatoes the hospital needed to feed the masses. The only thing between starvation and getting fed was me – and I had no idea how I was to prepare and present the product that the kitchen expected by eleven that day. The main piece of gadgetry, taking up most of the floor space, was the spud peeler. It had a large revolving drum, with hoppers, feeders and a maze of other bits and pieces that might have looked more suitable bolted on to a spaceship. Turning it on was no problem, as a large green knob mounted on the wall solved that issue, immediately transforming the room from peacefulness into vibrating chaos.

Humping a massive bag over to the machine, I dumped in about a quarter of a ton of large, filthy potatoes. I looked into the drum (feeling quite proud that I had managed so far on my own) and was dismayed to see that it resembled an unstable bog suffering an earthquake. It was nothing but a heaving mass of black soil, potato skins and black, oblong lumps being pushed up and down as they slowly rotated. I knew then that I had forgotten something. Water.

I rushed over to the taps and turned on the large valves. The tank was immediately flooded, but it was too late because the soil and peelings had already clogged up the drains. I should have had the water running from the start of the operation. Using a large, flat shovel, it took me about an hour to clean up the mess and, by the time I had finished, the potatoes had been filed down to the size of small eggs. When I presented my offerings to the chef, he just commented, 'Jesus, you must be the new fellow, what?'

I had to join the union, or at least that's what Tommy (the union representative, also known as Brother Slim) told me when he called to sign me up and collect my subscription. I became a 'brother' and had to listen for about an hour while he lectured me on all of the 'don'ts' that I must heed in the course of my working day.

'Right sonny, now, those bastards will try and get you to do bleeden' work that we in the union have been struggling against for bluudy years.'

'Like what?' I said, thinking it was a smart question, but it seemed to stump him.

'Well, Jaysus, let me bleeden' think. Christ, youse put me off me stride there.'

'Well,' I began, my mind racing to come up quickly with the daftest situation I could rustle up on the spot. 'I was just wondering what sort of job I should refuse to do, you know. Suppose I am walking by, minding my own business, and the matron, in passing, asks me to walk her dog, like, should I tell her to fuck off and send her off to see you?'

'Jaysus, are youse thick or wha'?' he said, while struggling to lift one of his short, fat legs so that he could rest it on top of a bag of spuds. 'Take these bleeden' bags, wha'? How heavy do youse think they are?'

'Well it's written on the bag under your foot, 100 cwt.'

'Right. Now youse have it. Here's an example of what we've been talking about.'

The man had obviously lost his marbles, but the good news was that nobody was going to interrupt this conversation and tell me to get back to work. That sort of attitude might result in an all-out strike.

'For years, we in the union have been bleeden' struggling to stop this sort of exploitation of the worker. I mean, you shouldn't have to lift these on your own, you could put your bleeden' back out. Now we have been telling the man you have replaced, Spuds, that the union will back him if he doesn't get his helper and I will call an all-out strike.'

It seemed to me to be a wonder that the hospital

functioned at all with the attitude the union had regarding work. Here was this fellow being absolutely serious about having an 'assistant spud-bag lifter', whose only task would be to lift five or six bags a day. No wonder the Health Board was haemorrhaging money every year with the likes of those fellows dictating policy.

Promising Brother Slim that I would attend the next union meeting, I finally got rid of him. However, over the following months I was to have many visits from him. All of them dealing with complaints from fellow 'brother porters' about the amount of work I got through every day and the speed with which I carried out my various tasks. On one occasion I was even chastised for carrying too many X-rays over to Outpatients in one go. They were bulky, but light as a feather, and I was en route with about ten of them under each arm when I was apprehended by Brother Slim.

'Now Jaysus, sonny, haven't I been telling you about this, wha'? Jaysus, what will bleeden' happen when tosser Riley comes back off his holliers all fecking relaxed, right? These capitalist bastards will then expect him to carry the same amount, rite? Jaysus, what are you trying to do, feck up the whole system that Connolly died for, wha'?'

That was the day he became my mortal enemy. I told the fat slob to 'go fuck yourself and shove your union up your own arse if you don't like it'. I couldn't see the logic in making three trips when I could do it in one, and it wasn't my fault if tosser Riley should have been sacked years ago for being the lazy git that he was. He kept away from me after that, but still constantly tried to get me into trouble with the matron. He needn't have bothered as I was managing to do that quite successfully all on my own.

After the two-week kitchen stint, I took over the porter's job at Hospital 3, the geriatrics unit where my mother was nursing. My main job was to haul out the soiled laundry in the morning and replace it with the newly washed. As most of the geriatrics never left their beds, the volume, weight and smell from the linen bags was terrible and it was a job best done without a hangover. There was a special lift designated for this task, which ran the three floors, but it was placed at the furthest end of the building. Every day I had to drag, carry, or hump these bags down the long corridors to this service lift. I then deposited them in a loading bay where, once a day, they were collected by the laundry van, which returned later with the clean stuff.

I would then repeat the process all over again in reverse: but since the new bags were fresh smelling and relatively light this was the easy part. It was the weight of the soiled bags that caused me the problems. Obviously Brother Slim's attention had not been brought to bear on this situation, otherwise he probably would have issued a union warning to the patients: 'Now Jaysus, wha'? One crap a day is all youse lot are entitled to, rite? Otherwise, it's an all-out bleeden' strike and youse can all go and wash yer own sheets.'

The plan I came up with was a lot simpler and quicker. Running down the length of the building along the corridors were old-fashioned, large, sash windows, which opened onto a well-manicured lawn. So, instead of lugging the bags along the corridors, I simply chucked them out of the windows onto the lawn. I had already spoken to the van driver and he didn't care where he collected them from. After a few days I had it down to a fine art; the trick was to make sure nobody caught me. On removing a bag from the storage room, I would drag it over to the nearest window, check left and right to make sure that the coast was clear, open the window, toss out the bag, and then close the window again. The whole operation took less that five seconds. Then I'd move on to the next room and repeat the procedure. The geriatrics thought it was all great entertainment and some of them even applauded with glee when they heard the bags thumping off the lawn, especially the really heavy ones from the third floor, because they sounded like howitzer shells exploding on impact.

That was how I came to have my first interview with the matron. She just happened to be passing under a window one fine morning, walking her dog, when one of my missiles landed within a few feet of her. It scared the living daylights out of her and caused the woman to scream her head off in fright. When I heard the fracas I looked out of the window, thinking that one of the geriatrics had escaped on walk-about. So I bolted down the stairs with the intention of retrieving the escapee, but instead I ran headlong into the matron, now fully composed and intent on retribution.

Within hours of the incident the word had travelled throughout the place and I became something of a celebrity. With every telling the events were exaggerated more and more and I was quickly dubbed 'matron killer'. Brother Slim even came to see me to warn me that if I had any grievance in future, I must go through official union channels and was not to take matters into my own hands again. However, since I had had a problem with that 'bitch of a matron', he would leave it go this time. My mother was definitely not amused.

As penance the matron gave me a week's work as night attendant in the morgue and I left her office to her flippant remark: 'As the building has no windows, I fail to see how you can get yourself into trouble there.' I didn't like this new job one bit, as it scared the wits out of me and my fertile imagination worked overtime. It was a relatively small, purpose-built, single-storey building with an outer office; the dead bodies, or 'stiffs', were held in refrigerated drawers in the main room at the back. My task was quite simple and straightforward and very similar to the role of a receptionist in a small hotel. The porter in attendance had to check in the arrivals and log out the departures; but, since none of this activity happened during the night when I was on duty, I just had to make sure that nobody tried to get in or out without proper approval. That is why I kept the door between the 'stiffs' and me firmly locked, in case any of them took the notion to leave. Nearly all of the temporary residents in my care were elderly people who had died of old age. After the pubs closed in the evenings I could get quite a flurry of relatives pitching up to see 'auld aunt June' who had passed away that day, 'God bless her soul, may she rest in peace.' These would be the same relatives who had neglected to visit her while she was still alive; they would arrive smelling like the Guinness brewery, shedding crocodile tears and with one eye firmly fixed on the will.

Three days into the job a Mary Quigley was delivered into my care. She was an eighty-year-old lady who had passed away that morning. The nuns did the 'laying out' of the bodies and they always tied the corpse's hands together above the chest in the universal position of prayer. At around midnight I was woken from my snoozing by the pounding of fists on the door and I nearly jumped out of my skin, thinking that it was one of the stiffs trying to break out. I rushed to the front door with the intention of bolting far away into the night, only to rush headlong into a large group standing outside who had been responsible for making the racket. Apparently they had been pounding on the door for over ten minutes trying to wake me up. White as a ghost and shaking like a leaf from the fright, I told them that, in fact, I had not been asleep, but engaged in my nightly round of the bodies.

'Ha, Jesus, Mick, next he'll be telling us that he was playing cards with them,' one commented as I led them into the office. There were nine people in total, middle-aged and all polluted with the drink. Attempting to re-establish my authority over them, I pretended to check my list for the deceased's name. 'Ah, here she is, a Mrs Mary Quigley, passed away this morning. Are you all the next of kin?'

'What?' said one of the group, who was slightly older and had elected himself the spokesperson. I retreated a few steps from the smell of undiluted Guinness that was wafting over me.

'Are . . . all . . . of . . . you . . . relatives?'

'Jesus, who the fock do you bleeden' think we are, bleeden' body snatchers? Ha, ha.' Which brought howls of drunken laughter from the rest of the mob crowded around me in the small office.

'Right, follow me.' I unlocked the dividing door and led them into the morgue, strolling halfway down before stopping in front of a large, stainless-steel drawer bearing her name. I had been instructed to open the drawer slowly and then step back out of the way, allowing the relatives some sort of privacy. There was never any of the usual stuff that you see on TV, such as the attendant removing a sheet from face. That was not our job; if they wanted to view the body (which most of them didn't anyway), they could pull back the white sheet themselves. In this case three things happened simultaneously when I yanked open the drawer. (Perhaps, in retrospect, I used a bit more force than necessary.) There came a loud ripping noise, quite similar to that of a large sheet being torn in half, a heavy thud – and an ear-piercing scream.

None of this encouraged me to hang around in search of an explanation. I was up and out of the room, through the office, and halfway across the grounds before I stopped to draw air into my heaving lungs – but I intended to keep going until I reached the safety of my own house. At that moment I was almost run down by the mob of relatives who were right on my heels and set on overtaking me. The ensuing row between us made such a commotion that we woke up half of the hospital, resulting in security being called. And that, of course, was how the matron found out about the whole sorry affair.

For the second time in as many days I stood in her office giving her an account of the previous night's happenings. By the time I had finished my account, she had developed a nervous tick in her right cheek muscle. When I finally left her office I could have sworn that I could hear her howling with laughter, convincing me that perhaps she had a sense of humour after all. But I felt it was all very well for her, as she hadn't been there. It would take me weeks to get over the shock.

For when I had opened the drawer back there in the morgue, old Mary had sprung to life. Of course she hadn't really, but it had appeared that way because the nuns had been a bit over-zealous in tying her hands together. As I pulled open the drawer, her hands must have caught on the top of the cabinet, causing the whole sheet to move violently as if she was about to jump up. The loud ripping noise was somebody in the group farting with fright. The heavy thud was another member of the group fainting, and the ear-piercing scream was self-explanatory. The violent row on the lawn had been because the relatives wanted me to go back in and retrieve the body of their fallen member. I argued that it was their re-sponsibility, since that person was actually their own mother. We only calmed down somewhat when their fallen member staggered out to report that 'Old Mary is still quite dead'. That little uproar made the rounds of the hospital even faster than the story that was now referred to as 'the case of the mis-aimed laundry bag'.

Towards the end of the summer I was posted to Hospital 7, with responsibility for taking patients up to the various wards after they had been admitted, as well as collecting and delivering blood samples, X-rays and all the bits and pieces that the doctors fancied testing. Hospital 7 also housed the main records department of every person who had been admitted in the past few years. The fetching and delivering of records for patients who had been admitted into one of the other hospitals was another role of mine.

One evening, finding myself alone amongst the rows and rows of files, I decided to check if any of the records held details of my parent. There was, in fact, one slim file on my father, which had been compiled by the doctor in charge of the ward during his most recent visit to the hospital. I appropriated the two hand-written pages (ignoring all of the information relating to his medical condition) and later that evening I read them before setting them on fire. I had realised that he was more than qualified to act the maggot when he chose and (before reading those papers) had actually believed that I knew everything of which he was capable. However, this new evidence took the overall medal and I can only assume that he must have been heavily on the bottle during that stay in the hospital.

The notes were basically an account of his actions with regard to the nursing staff. Most of the comments related to various occasions on which he had been found galloping around the wards, stark naked, proudly displaying his full erection while in hot pursuit of the nurses – and demanding that they come back and be administered to. Considering the position that he held in the establishment, I was at first embarrassed for him. And then the shame set in, causing me to blush bright red, when I thought about how many other people must have read these pages, knowing that I was his son. Well, I was going to make sure that nobody would ever read them again, because I was definitely not going to bear the sins of my father.

September finally arrived and with it, on the same day, came
three letters, all bearing bad news in one form or another. I
had been working the evening shift as a switchboard operator
over in the Coombe Hospital, which must have been affiliated
in some way with St James's. I had a tiny little office and a
switchboard that was surely one of the oldest still operational
in the country. This contraption took up a complete wall and
all calls, in or out of the building, had to come through this
monstrosity. When an incoming call arrived, or if somebody
on the inside wanted to phone out, a small cup fell down to
announce the line or extension that was seeking attention. I
then made the connection using a bunch of spring-loaded
plugs that pulled out of the tabletop at the base of the
exchange. When the call ended the silver cup would fly back
up, at which I had to unplug the connections between that
extension and the outside line. When it was busy the table
resembled a bird's nest, with criss-crossing wires plugged into
the board every which way. Late in the evenings when all went
quiet, I discovered that from my switchboard I could dial up
two separate outside numbers and connect them to each other
while still being able to listen in. My favourite joke was to
connect two different police stations and then sit back to listen
to the fruits of my work.

'Hello, Kilmainham Garda Station.'

While, at exactly the same time, 'Hello, Rathmines Garda
Station, Sergeant Murphy speaking.' Short pause. Then,
'Hello? Who is this?'

'This is Kilmainham Garda station, you rang us, what do
you want?'

'What do you mean, we rang you? Now stop this
nonsense, you rang us.'

'Murphy, is this is your idea of a joke? We're busy here,

not like you. Apparently you have time to sit on your arses and make calls wasting our time.'

'Who is this? Is that you McCarthy, you focker, you rang us you Cork hoorer.'

And so it would continue, with both of them getting madder and madder at each other, until I eventually pulled the plugs, allowing each to think that the other had hung up. After waiting about thirty minutes, I would repeat the process all over again. However, that evening after opening my mail, I couldn't even motivate myself to start annoying Garda stations. The first letter contained the results of my Leaving Cert. exam. Out of the eight subjects I had sat, I had passed six, failing French and, of course, Irish. So no university for me.

The next letter was from the hospital thanking me for filling in over the summer months. What a great fellow I had been and all of that rubbish, but as all of the holidays had now been taken, they no longer required my services. Since they were sure I had done well in my Leaving, they wished me every success in joining the university of my choice and they looked forward to having me back for the following year's summer fill-in.

It was the last letter that bothered me the most and it was from Gina. I had written to say that I could meet with her on the following weekend. Her reply told me that that she couldn't make it, as her mother had grounded her. In a sense, while disappointing, the news didn't bother me much. It was the signature at the bottom that instilled a feeling of complete loss, building in the pit of my stomach. Instead of her customary 'with all of my love', this one just read 'lots of love'. And even before I had reached the end of the letter I sensed a change in her writing, suggesting that perhaps Gina was tiring of a friendship that took place courtesy of the post office. Or maybe she had found somebody else who was able to offer a bit more than badly spelt words on a piece of paper. Whatever the reason, I sensed a change that was blowing an ill wind in my direction.

The only bit of good news around this time was that the parents were moving into their new house in Malahide. Two days later, with all of our furniture packed into the rear of a removals van, they departed to wreak havoc on their new and unsuspecting neighbours.

For one of the few times in my life I had stood up to the mother and refused, point-blank, to leave our house until I had to, because it would be at least another six months before the Health Board moved in. She seemed to think that if she left me only the bare necessities of life, in a few days I would (as she put it) 'see sense and come running after us'. I was left a mattress, some bedclothes, an old two-drawer sideboard, one pot and pan, cup, knife and fork, and one plate. So, in essence, I didn't actually leave home, my parents did.

That first night, as I walked through the house with my footsteps echoing around the empty rooms, I felt a sense of peace and tranquillity, although I was looking at a very uncertain future. The house felt sad, as if it was mourning the departure of people it had sheltered within its walls for nearly twenty years; regardless of all of the rows, those walls must have remembered the good times as well.

Closing my eyes as I strolled along the entrance hallway, I visualised the grandparents' comings and goings, and it seemed as if it had been only yesterday that old Claus went out this way for his daily walk.

Catherine's first steps had also been taken along this hallway, although there were now bare boards where the carpet had once been laid. It was almost as if I could hear her laughter as she waited by the hall door for my return from school every day.

The wallpaper was still marked where Boy-o-Boy had knocked against it on his drunken way to the floor as I let him in that very first night. Looking into the kitchen, now in darkness, I felt as if I had gone back in time and was once again that little boy rushing downstairs after counting the money on my first Christmas Eve assisting in the shop. I felt that the energies of all of the people who had helped out throughout the years had returned to bid a silent farewell to a shop that had been known as 'Everybody's' of Inchicore.

I placed the mattress on the floor of what had been the parents' room, simply because it was smaller and, I imagined, would not be as cold as my own. When I finally crawled under the covers, I knew that, on this night, sleep would be a long time coming. Listening to the street noises filtering in through the window (comforting sounds, for they were the noises I had grown up with), I wondered what would become of me.

On the plus side, I had money, as I had been able to save quite a lot over the past few months. Enough at least for the immediate future. Just as well since, come next Thursday, I would have no job. I had failed my Leaving, so I had no qualifications worth talking about. I definitely had to scratch out looking for a white-collar job, as those companies wanted to train candidates who could produce a Leaving Certificate with a bunch of honours littering the page. No, I wouldn't waste my time there.

My grand idea of taking over the shop and developing it into a good business had come to nothing, and it was beginning to look as if the only woman I cared about was losing interest in me as well. I felt the hardness of the floor through the mattress as I waited for sleep and, over and over, experienced a desperate urge to simply hop on my bike and head down the country to see Gina. But then what would I do? The money would run out and I would have to throw myself on the mercy of Matty and his family. Not to mention the fact that I had considered this scenario in the past and had concluded that it could not possibly work. I searched my memory for some redeeming note in Gina's last letter. Something that suggested things might not be as bad as I feared. And then, finally, I drifted into a dream-filled slumber.

∞

With a start I came back to the present and took in my surroundings. It was over now: even the last night here was over. And I was stiff with the cold because I had fallen asleep, propped against the back wall of our kitchen. Mice had been sampling my abandoned chips, now scattered in all directions. Stretching, I forced stiff limbs into movement. I was feeling a fair bit better after those night hours with the ghosts from my past – and calmer about everything that had happened. It was if I had put myself through an exorcism and had come out the far side stronger as a result. I could now accept most of the past, or at least Catherine's death and the court case. There was really no one to blame for her death. It had been an accident, pure and simple, brought on by a sequence of seemingly random events that had lead us irrevocably towards that fateful day back in 1966. Isn't that how accidents happen?

To a certain extent I could also accept the parents' bitter disappointment at the lack of 'compo' and the way they had taken refuge in the bottle. But there were still certain episodes I would never understand on my own, and with which, one day, I would have to confront them. I could not help feeling that somewhere along the way they had abandoned me, acting in a manner that was self-centred, bordering on careless and grossly neglectful. I felt that I had been reborn at the age of ten;

a rebirth which had turned me into a completely different person. I was now a complete loner with a cavalier attitude towards life in general. What this new person would eventually become, well, I could only wait and see.

As for the parents, I knew now that they would never find inner peace or come to terms with what had happened. I believed they were fated to spend the rest of their lives blaming each other for something that was not their fault. Always assuming that they didn't kill each other in the meantime; if I remembered correctly, there was at least one more statue of some saint or another knocking about the house. Finally I realised, with a conviction that surprised me, that I could never move back into their environment again.

I had spent the last five months working as a dock runner for a shipping company operating out of Bluebell Industrial Estate and, while the job was interesting because I had visited some of the shadier pubs in Dublin's docklands, the money was terrible. Which reminded me, I had a job interview coming up the next week with a shipping company on Eden Quay and they were offering £27 a week to the lucky candidate. All I had to do was to ensure I got the job by being more creative at the interview than the other candidates and I would be able to get a flat in Rathmines. Meanwhile, I would call David to see if he could offer me a room until I sorted myself out.

And that brought me back to my problem with Gina. I had seen her twice in the last six months and, when we had met, it had been as if nothing had changed between us. It was the time apart that was destroying us and there wasn't a lot I could do about that for the present. But there was a bank holiday coming up and I would write to her this day to see if she was free to meet up with me.

Somewhere out there had to be a solution. I felt within

myself a vast ability and a positive energy crying out to be released, if only I could find the right catalyst.

∞

Disappointment was something to which I was well accustomed by now. When I called David, he said he couldn't oblige me with a room or, to be more precise, his parents couldn't. Gina wrote back immediately to say that she was busy for the weekend. Then, to cap it all, I suddenly remembered that the fellow who got me the job interview had also warned me to turn up wearing a suit. That meant I would have to get myself into Burton's on Dame Street and buy one on the never-never.

It was a lovely, sunny Friday evening and, instead of being halfway to County Cork, I was sitting at the traffic lights at the bottom of Talbot Street. I was pondering my problems and feeling sorry for myself when my eye caught the smiling face of a gurrier astride a 350cc Triumph – he was clearly after a dice. As I stared at his leering face, it suddenly seemed as if he were to blame for all of my problems. So, when the lights turned green, I slipped the clutch and shot up the street like a bullet fired from a gun. Who the hell did he think he was anyway, trying to take on a BSA 500?

Feck, he was still there on my inside as the noise from the two machines on full throttle reverberated up and down the road, causing heads to turn. I was still accelerating, determined to reach O'Connell Street before him, and we were just entering the narrow section at the junction of Marlborough Street when a flash of red entered my peripheral vision to the right.

I came to, crumpled up against the entrance doors of a pub about a hundred yards down Marlborough Street with a bunch of Moore Street vendors peering at me. For a fleeting moment I thought they were going to flog me some bangers.

'Jaysus, sonny, are youse all right? Me and Mary thought the bleeden' pub had been hit by a corporation truck, put the fear of the Lord God into us. Jaysus, was youse in that crash?' She reached up and adjusted the multicoloured rollers sticking out from under the scarf that held them in place.

'I don't know, I just got here myself.' It was the only reply I could come up with on short notice, as my head was reeling from whatever had hit me. 'What happened?'

'Holy God, would youse look, there's bleeden' carnage up there, bodies everywhere. Here, take this brandy, t'will do ya good. I couldn't touch it now mesel' as me nerves are gone.'

My right hand wouldn't work, so I took the proffered drink with a shaking left hand. Amazingly my crash helmet was still attached to my head, but the chinstrap had broken.

She continued with her crash report. 'Jaysus, ha, ha. Youse can always say that youse ran into an important person, ha, ha, isn't that rite, Mary? That's Maureen Potter youse lot crashed into and her on the way to the Abbey. I'm glad I don't have tickets for her show tonight. Ahh, but God love us, have ya seen the other two poor craturs? Jaysus they'd be better off dead.'

The other two, I wondered? Where did this third person come from? Using the wall for support, I pulled myself up slowly to a standing position and took stock of what the two women were ranting on about. For the first time I could see the ambulance parked only a few feet from me, but the attendants were busy over in the middle of Talbot Street, bending over two stretchers. A red car was embedded in the wall of a shop front at the junction and I could see my bike's front wheel buried in the now demolished passenger door. But how I had ended up down this street I had no idea. There were police, doctors and firemen everywhere as if a bomb had gone off and the car looked as if it had been run over by a steamroller.

'Sonny, are youse going to drink tha' bleeden' brandy after I gave it ya, or just sniff it? Haw.'

Before I could think of a suitable answer, a man who had rushed down the street wearing a pair of cycle clips joined us. But before he could open his mouth to say a word he was accosted by one of my minders.

'Jim, are them two dead or wha'?'

Before Jim answered her, he gave me a look of sheer amazement and asked, 'Jaysus young fella, was youse driving the big bike sticking outta the car door? How d'ya end up here anyway? Fuck, youse are bleeden' lucky to be alive. Youse wanna see the other two.'

There they were again with the other two. 'What other two?' I roared, as my head was still ringing.

'Jaysus sonny, will youse let him talk? Shure, can't youse see he's busting to tell us? Go on, Jim, tell us. This fella looks all righ' for the moment, are you feeling all righ', sonny?'

'Well, the poor fecker driving th'other bike landed up in O'Connell Street, and him with his right leg missing. Look at it, lying there against the front of the car.'

'Jaysus, Mary and Joseph,' chimed the two women in unison and simultaneously blessed themselves as if they were controlled by the same puppeteer.

'Agh Jaysus, Jim, I need another ball of malt.' And with that Janie roared back in through the pub doors, 'Billy, bring us out three whiskeys, quick. Before I get an attack of me nerves again. Young fella, d'ya want another brandy?'

'But that's only the start of it,' continued Jim, 'The driver of the car . . . '

'That's your wan, ya know, the axtress,' interrupted Mary.

'Jaysus, will you bleeden' let him finish before the amblenance men take the lot of us away and lock us up in the mental hospital?' retorted Janie, as she took the new drinks from the barman who had joined us on the street.

'Well, after she was hit by the two bikes . . .'

'What do you mean – hit by the two bikes?' I spluttered in exasperation. 'She came flying out of the street up there, straight through the Stop sign without stopping.'

'Well, that's as may be, but it didn't stop her from swerving across the road, mounting the footpath and crushing another poor fella against the shop wall just up there, and I think that fella's had it. Shure, they've sent for the priest an' all.'

'Ah, God love us, look, look, Mary, they're stretchering them down now. Quick sonny, youse better get in the amblenance as well. Youse don't look too good, youse've just gone a funny colour.'

A funny colour? While I had been listening to the story I had undertaken a self-examination. My collarbone was broken and popping up and down under my fingers. My right arm was definitely broken and the wrist didn't feel any better. As I started walking towards the back of the ambulance I couldn't help feeling a bout of self-pity. 'Janie, thanks for the drink, I owe you one. It's just the perfect bloody ending to the fecked-up week I've had. It's been nothing but one problem after another. I suppose, on the bright side, I had no place to stay – but the last place in the fecking world I thought I would end up is a bed at St James's Hospital.'

As the ambulance sped away with the sirens going, I had to smile for the first time in agreement with Janie's response.

'Jaysus sonny, you think youse're hard done by? Look at them poor souls lying there alongside ya, they're definitely having a bleeden' bad week. Agh sure, God love 'em.'